SAVING GENERAL WASHINGTON

JEREMY P. TARCHER/PENGUIN

A MEMBER OF

PENGUIN GROUP (USA) INC.

NEW YORK

SAVING GENERAL WASHINGTON

THE RIGHT WING ASSAULT
ON AMERICA'S FOUNDING PRINCIPLES

J. R. NORTON

ILLUSTRATIONS BY DEREK EVERNDEN

JEREMY P. TARCHER/PENGUIN
Published by the Penguin Group
Penguin Group (USA) Inc., 375 Hudson Street, New York, New York 10014, USA • Penguin Group (Canada),
90 Eglinton Avenue East, Suite 700, Toronto, Ontario M4P 2Y3, Canada (a division of Pearson Penguin
Canada Inc.) • Penguin Books Ltd, 80 Strand, London WC2R 0RL, England • Penguin Ireland,
25 St Stephen's Green, Dublin 2, Ireland (a division of Penguin Books Ltd) • Penguin Group (Australia),
250 Camberwell Road, Camberwell, Victoria 3124, Australia (a division of Pearson Australia Group Pty Ltd) •
Penguin Books India Pvt Ltd, 11 Community Centre, Panchsheel Park, New Delhi–110 017, India •
Penguin Group (NZ), Cnr Airborne and Rosedale Roads, Albany, Auckland 1310, New Zealand
(a division of Pearson New Zealand Ltd) • Penguin Books (South Africa) (Pty) Ltd,
24 Sturdee Avenue, Rosebank, Johannesburg 2196, South Africa

Penguin Books Ltd, Registered Offices:
80 Strand, London WC2R 0RL, England

Most Tarcher/Penguin books are available at special quantity discounts for bulk purchase for sales promotions,
premiums, fund-raising, and educational needs. Special books or book excerpts also can be created to fit specific
needs. For details, write Penguin Group (USA) Inc. Special Markets, 375 Hudson Street, New York, NY 10014.

Library of Congress Cataloging-in-Publication Data

Norton, James R.
Saving General Washington : the right wing assault on America's founding principles
J. R. Norton ; illustrations by Derek Evernden.
p.   cm.
ISBN 1-58542-486-2
1. United States—Politics and government—2001–   2. Bush, George W. (George Walker), 1946–
3. Conservatism—United States.   4. Political science—United States—History—18th century.
5. United States—Politics and government—1775–1783.   I. Title.
E902.N67   2006   2006040934
973.3102'07—dc22

Printed in the United States of America
1   3   5   7   9   10   8   6   4   2

Book design by Stephanie Huntwork

While the author has made every effort to provide accurate telephone numbers and Internet addresses at the time
of publication, neither the publisher nor the author assumes any responsibility for errors, or for changes that occur
after publication. Further, the publisher does not have any control over and does not assume any responsibility for
author or third-party websites or their content.

FOR BECCA

CONTENTS

A little patience, and we shall see the reign of witches pass over, their spells dissolve, and the people, recovering their true sight, restore their government to its true principles.

—Thomas Jefferson, letter to John Taylor, 1798

Excuse me—when you're done with that [copy of Common Sense*], would you send it to George W. Bush?*

—Coffee shop patron, to the author, September 2005

INTRODUCTION

The spirit of the times may alter, will alter. Our rulers will become corrupt, our people careless. . . . From the conclusion of this war, we shall be going down hill. . . . The shackles, therefore, which shall not be knocked off at the conclusion of this war, will remain on us long, will be made heavier and heavier, till our rights shall revive or expire in a convulsion.

—Thomas Jefferson, *Notes on the State of Virginia,* 1787

WE, THE AMERICAN PEOPLE, need to do a little quiet reflection.

We live in an age when a single political party—one that openly labors to dominate the entire political system—controls the big three: the executive branch, the legislative branch, and the judiciary. Checks and balances never looked so thoroughly unchecked and unbalanced. The number-one qualification for public service jobs, ranging from the head of FEMA to a seat on the Supreme Court, is enthusiastic personal loyalty to the president. A large and influential group of American legislators—at a time when the national debt has ballooned beyond recognition and we seem to be involved in one of those awkward "land war" things—has decided that the number-one national priority should be to put a stop to gay marriage. Honest debate is under the boot of the ad hominem attack. Balanced government is under mortar attack. "Faith-based" initiatives are ascendant.

Twelve years after the Newt Gingrich revolution railed against corrupt "big" government, Republicans have boldly defied their own rhetoric to become the corrupt party of big government, increasingly defined by a bloated budget deficit and the fiscal tentacles of Jack Abramoff. And six years after one of the most successful two-term presidencies in American history, the party of Clinton has been transformed from a pragmatic powerhouse headed by a charismatic Southerner to a mostly listless group of nobodies headed by, well, nobody.

It's difficult to remember that we live in a nation founded by revolutionaries whose progressive views on science, religion, and government shocked the frilly britches off the Western world. Their progressive—indeed, earth-shattering—writing and thinking explain and dramatize like nothing else in history how America has gone completely off the rails, and how it can make a comeback as inspiring as the training montage in *Rocky IV.* Seasoned old soldiers, these dusty mercenaries are absolutely relentless in their logic, their honesty, their opposition to tyranny, and their pragmatic belief in good, clean, representative government.

These days, when you hear the Founding Fathers mentioned in public, it's for one of two reasons: someone is saying something boring about history, or a Republican office-holder is lying to the public.

Thanks to generations of deification through educational cartoons, mandatory social studies workbooks, profiles on small-denomination currency, and other not-very-compelling public appearances, the Founding Fathers are widely regarded as duller than C-SPAN.

The truth—as informed by the actual historical record—is that these guys were more dangerous and exciting than Che Guevara, Joe Strummer, and 50 Cent combined. They included a former cabinet secretary killed in a gunfight with a sitting vice president (Alexander Hamilton and Aaron Burr). They included a hard-charging fighter who risked his life on the front lines of battle and then, when the public demanded he be made king, demurred (George Washington). And they included a salty old playboy who, between inventions and constitutional conventions, fraternized the hell out of Western Europe's womenfolk (Benjamin Franklin).

We now enjoy the leadership skills of a pampered oil heir elevated to the presidency by the Supreme Court; a vice president who has one chubby paw in industry, and the other in the legislature that regulates—or refuses to regulate—that industry; and shameless draft-dodgers who send Americans to their deaths in an ideological war sold under false pretenses. Just as we enjoy "Intelligent Design" and bad science prostituting itself to the demands of wealthy corporations, and the torture of prisoners, a practice formerly regarded as barbaric and un-American.

The revolutionary ass-kickers who founded this country saw this coming a million miles away, centuries before the first monstrous claw touched the asphalt. Take war—in describing bad reasons for declaring war, John Jay, the first chief justice of the United States, wrote about "a thirst for military glory, revenge for personal affronts, or private compacts to aggrandize or support their particular families or partisans." He was talking about why kings embark upon wars that are "not sanctified by justice or the voice and interests of his people." But were Jay speaking these words today, wearing a three-piece suit and sans wig, he could just as well be talking about that "Mission Accomplished" banner flapping in the Pacific Ocean breeze while an American president in a flight suit gives the thumbs-up.

What about political loyalty? In talking about the dangers of insisting on political loyalty instead of the public good, and silencing political debate, James Madison wrote: "Liberty is to faction what air is to fire, an [element] without which it instantly expires." In honor of this precept, Bush press secretary Ari Fleischer famously urged Americans, after 9/11, "to watch what they say, watch what they do."

And the Founding Fathers foresaw what happens when "no new taxes" supplants "good government" as the law of the land—Hamilton warned of civil chaos caused by a government starved of revenue and unable to address new crises.

But modern Republicans have made a smart bet. They're wagering that Americans in general (and young people in particular) have gotten so far from their own history that the ideals the Founding Fathers originally stood for can be pushed out of public life, invoking them only to say: "They would have been on *our* side. America's Founding Fathers would have wanted more religion in government! They wanted a strong executive branch! They hated progressive interpretations of law by the Supreme Court! They would have been appalled by referring to foreign precedent in American legal decisions!"

Bullshit.

The more you learn about the Founders, the more broad and

powerful parallels emerge between their practical and ultimately revolutionary political ideas, and those of modern progressives.

America's colonial revolutionaries believed in the dignity of human life, not torturing prisoners—or even slaves. They believed in reason and strenuous debate, not "faith" in politically active religious leaders and the crushing of dissent. They believed in checks and balances—in fact, they created the damn things. They believed in cautious and judicious intervention in foreign affairs, not a reckless war fought for a mix of economic and utopian causes.

The Founders and the Framers weren't saints—their failure to obliterate the evil of slavery planted the seeds of the American Civil War, and their clashing visions for America's progress set in motion wheels of political conflict that still turn today.

But taken as a whole, America's founders fought to break free from authoritarianism, not to impose it. And if they got a "deferment" from the colonial army, they couldn't make it in American politics, period. There were no "Schooner Ship Vets" to bail them out by making George Washington look like a deceptive medal-hound. And there weren't any sweetheart deals between Washington and Ye Olde Whale Oil Supply Company.

Against all odds, there's an idea, promulgated by the likes of Bill O'Reilly, that the Republican Party somehow best captures "traditionalist" ideals. But the modern conservative movement—and by this I mean the guys in power, and the guys in the think tanks and corporate lobbies handing them the bills to pass and buzz phrases to utter—are about as revolutionary as anyone since Washington, Jefferson, Hamilton, and their brethren. Only this time, it's a revolution against reason, fairness, and clean government.

It's time for a showdown. It's time for the Spirit of '76 to come face-to-face with the rotten fruits of *Gore v. Bush*. In fact, I'd like to think that if George Washington's zombie came face-to-face with our current president, he'd say something like this:

ZOMBIE GEORGE WASHINGTON, FOUNDER AND FIRST PRESIDENT OF THE UNITED STATES OF AMERICA: George W. Bush, you cowardly Fece, you have thoroughly tarnished the liberty that the Revolution wrought. I hereby challenge you to a deadly duel of Chainsaws.

In reality, of course, it would be a far more lengthy and nuanced discussion. And Washington, who lived a life of decorum, humility, and decency, would choose his words carefully. Whether it would all end in a bloody spray of severed limbs somewhere on a green Virginia hillside is a question best settled by more meticulous and serious historians than I.

It's this discussion, between America's founders and the politicians of our era, that must be started as soon as possible. And because the original Framers are dead, it is we—Americans with an interest in honest debate, factual accuracy, and pragmatism and a sincere wish that the country not self-destruct—who need to get the words and ideas of the Framers back into common circulation.

First, a couple of caveats about this book. It is not an exhaustive compilation of the Founders' Greatest Hits. It is not a scholarly work of history, nor is it a work of revisionism. Instead, it uses the historical record to set our current political leaders, and the state of our government, in stark relief against the men who designed this "last, best hope of earth," the United States of America. You'll meet the men I like to call the Founding Badasses—guys like Hamilton, Washington, Franklin, Thomas Paine, Samuel

Adams, John Adams, James Madison, and others. They were the first progressives—they were dangerously revolutionary—and it's time for their modern descendants to reclaim their legacy.

In the process, the comparison between the lives and principles of the Founders and the lives and principles of the conservative movement in general and the Bush administration in particular illustrates just how far we've departed from the brilliant ideas and the core values America was built on and, I hope, will inspire us, in a small way, to take up the mantle of the Founders again. In that sense, *Saving General Washington* is a good old-fashioned polemic.

Every word from the Framers that appears here, every citation, every historical anecdote, can be invoked in the fight to return clean government and wholesome debate to a great country that is drowning under a tidal wave of misinformation, secrecy, and lies. It's time to pull back the curtain and talk about the contrast between the legitimate rock stars who so painstakingly put America together and the corporate tools who currently pull the strings of government.

We've got a lot of work to do. But we've got no right to complain about the integrity of the house; even if the roof is rotten, the foundation is rock-solid. Where other countries often have centuries of monarchy and tyranny to look back to, we have the Founders.

THE Alternate Universe DAILY SPECTATOR

NOVEMBER 27, 2001

Bin Laden, Lieutenant Captured at Tora Bora*

TORA BORA, AFGHANISTAN—In a battle dramatically overseen by the country's commander in chief, U.S. Marines and special forces stormed an Al Qaeda redoubt in eastern Afghanistan and seized most of Al Qaeda's leadership contingent before they could flee into neighboring Pakistan.

"I'd describe this operation as a ringing success," said a visibly exhausted and relieved President George W. Bush, talking to members of the press via a satellite video link. "We stepped it up at the right time, and we got our men. Justice has been served."

When it became clear that allied Afghan forces were losing their stomach for the fight against a fleeing enemy, Bush personally ordered U.S. forces to surround the mountain fortress of Tora Bora and make the assault.

"We knew the stakes of the battle," said Bush, "and we knew that this wasn't the Afghans' fight anymore—they'd gotten their country back, and they didn't give a lick whether Bin Laden was captured or not. It became America's fight. And we won it."

When asked why he took the unusual step of flying into Afghanistan as the Tora Bora showdown loomed, Bush cited the example of George Washington, who often personally led his troops against the British during the Revolutionary War.

"You didn't see me up front with a revolver," he said, giving his trademark chuckle, "but I wanted our boys to know that I'd be there in the mix, and that winning this battle was the most important thing to the American people."

Contrary to the president's words, a number of soldiers, speaking off the record, described the president making a surprise appearance in the midst of a firefight, blasting away with a pearl-handled revolver at a group of Al Qaeda militants taking shelter in a reinforced cave. "He didn't say much," said one sergeant who asked to remain anonymous. "He just patted me on the shoulder and said, 'Go get 'em, kid.' I thought I heard him mutter something about making up for lost time, and then, before I knew it, he'd advanced up into the [fray] with a team from Delta Force."

A defeated Bin Laden, speaking to reporters as he was frog-marched into Bagram airbase, had grudging words of praise for the American president. "Ya gotta hand it to the guy: He stepped it up in the fourth quarter and gave 110 percent. He was under the gun, and he put the pedal to the metal. He took his shot, and BOOM went the dynamite."

Experts and commentators alike were baffled by Bin Laden's mastery of American sports idioms.

*The newspaper articles and transcripts that appear between the chapters are works of satire.

ONE

A REVOLUTION REVERSED

The accumulation of all powers, legislative, executive, and judiciary, in the same hands . . . may justly be pronounced the very definition of tyranny.

—James Madison, *Federalist No. 47*

If this were a dictatorship, it would be a heck of a lot easier.

—George W. Bush, on his first trip to Washington, D.C., as president-elect, December 2000[1]

O NE LIABILITY—a glaring one, really—that all the Founders share is that they're dead. Being dead, they're unable to put in an appearance on *Crossfire* and object when their ideas and words are hijacked, perverted, and, perhaps worst, buried. Despite their meteoric brilliance while living, the Founders have started to fade away into empty caricatures of themselves.

It was only a matter of time before someone took advantage of that. The modern conservative movement has succeeded in using the Founders' words selectively to promote their own agenda. In the process, they've simultaneously managed to avoid nearly every piece of wise advice or instruction for principled government the Founders originally imparted.

Let's listen to President Bush invoke the Founding Fathers on January 22, 2001, in his Proclamation on the National Day of Prayer and Thanksgiving.

> President Jefferson also wrote, "The God who gave us life gave us liberty at the same time," and asked, "Can the liberties of a nation be secure when we have removed a conviction that these liberties are of God?" Indeed, it is appropriate to mark this occasion by remembering the words of President Jefferson and the examples of Americans of the past and today who in times of both joy and need turn to Almighty God in prayer.

Had the speech been about the actual lives and intentions of the Founding Fathers, and not part of a crusade to mix Christian prayers and fundamentalist ideology with public policy, Bush might have gone on to say the following:

> But we must also remember that it was Jefferson who, after his election to president, received a letter from a group of Baptists in Danbury, Connecticut. They asked the president to heal our nation's bitter wounds by proclaiming a national day of fasting and reconciliation much like the one I'm proclaiming today. Jefferson refused, telling them he couldn't do it without violating the U.S. Constitution and its First Amendment. He invoked the image of a "wall of separation between church and state."
>
> Poetic words.
>
> Years later, when asked to present a plan for public elementary schools to the Virginia legislatures, he proposed excluding

clergymen as school trustees, and forbidding religious instruction that violated the belief of any sect or denomination.

It's funny, standing here today, indebted as I am to wealthy and powerful fundamentalist religious figures such as Pat Robertson and James Dobson, to remember that Jefferson hated the involvement of the clergy in politics. The clergy, he wrote, had "perverted" Christianity "into an engine for enslaving mankind, a mere contrivance to filch wealth and power for themselves."

In fact, that famous inscription on the Jefferson Memorial— "I have sworn upon the altar of God eternal hostility against every form of tyranny over the mind of man"—is reference not to kings, but to the clergy of Philadelphia who were opposing his election as president. How about that.

So, on that wistfully ironic note, it's my pleasure to proclaim this national day of prayer and thanksgiving.

And here's the vice president, Dick Cheney, at the Abernathy Center in Oregon in September 2004, invoking George Washington in order to suggest that Iraq is on its way to stable, post-invasion freedom and tranquillity:

And I like to remind people of how long it took us from the time we declared our independence in 1776 until we finally had a Constitution in place and elected George Washington president and got started with the government that we all know and revere and the Constitution that we live under now was thirteen years. So this is a tough, difficult thing we're trying to do.

Slate's Fred Kaplan used the above quote as a springboard to make the point that the fractured, religiously and ethnically riven, and occupied Iraq in 2005 is about a million theoretical miles away from the united, liberated America of 1781. To a historian, the comparison was laughable, but Cheney made the comparison because:

(a) It sounds good to invoke the Founding Fathers when you're defending a disastrous war.

(b) Most people wouldn't think about it hard enough to question the parallel.

What is alarming is not simply the fact that the legacy of the Founding Fathers is regularly twisted when it's brought onto the national stage; it's that it's so rarely invoked in the first place during times of national crisis and struggle. Perhaps that's because our motives are no longer comparable.

The White House maintains a substantial online archive, which includes five years of information ranging from the declaration of hostilities against Iraq to a photo of a bemused-looking President Truman stroking a "pardoned" Thanksgiving turkey.

Type in a few searches having to do with the Bush White House:

- "George Washington": 314 results found

- "God": 1,993 results found

- "Thomas Jefferson": 165 results found

- "Ronald Reagan": 648 results found

- "Alexander Hamilton": 21 results found

- "Barney + dog": 862 results found

- "Founding Fathers": 38 results found

- "Easter egg": 24 results found

- "Clearing brush": 2 results found

- "Tom Paine": 0 results found

On the basis of this raw data, the big story isn't only that the Founding Fathers have been appropriated by all the wrong people. They've also been pushed into an unlit broom closet, left to chat awkwardly with former CIA director George Tenet and several thousand gay members of the armed services.

But raw search results are imprecise. For example: How many of the 165 results for Thomas Jefferson were actually examples of Bush or Cheney meaningfully invoking the Sage of Monticello? And how honest and accurate are those invocations?

After all, 165 is a substantial number. If Jefferson was brought into public discourse even half that many times, it would signify a real commitment to his legacy.

But once duplicate results, obscure budget documents, references to "Thomas Jefferson Day," and other miscellany were sorted out, there were about eight meaningful invocations of Thomas Jefferson during the Bush years. Consider the fact that Easter eggs have gotten more airtime than Jefferson at the Bush White House. Alexander Hamilton, the father of American government and the first secretary of the treasury, comes up twice. Washington merits about twenty mentions—the only Founding Father to break double digits. There are only five real references to inventor, diplomat, humanist, and journalist Benjamin Franklin. Founding firebrand Tom Paine doesn't merit a single mention—and despite his recent appearance on the *New York Times* bestseller list, John Adams snags one passing reference. James Madison, the father of the Constitution, gets two mentions—one of which is the president's saying that "graduating seniors at some of our leading colleges and universities . . . do not know that James Madison is the father of the Constitution."

It would be intriguing to spring that same question on Bush.

Q: Mr. President, can you tell us who James Madison was?

A: Why, sure I can. Mr. Madison. He was the . . . we call him "the father of the Constitution."

Q: What exactly does that mean?

A: Read a book about him last summer. Good book. Lot of pages, but I love history. Love to read. Okay, you there in the back?

Satire run amok? Not as amok as you might think. Here, right from the transcript, is George W. Bush at Lima Senior High School, in Ohio, on August 28, 2004:

STUDENT: Thanks for coming. I was just wondering what your favorite book is, because I'd like to read it.

BUSH: Book. That's a great question. Well, I (pause) the Bible. (Applause.) Hold on, hold on. I read the Bible. I like history. I read a lot of history. I'm not so sure this one will be appropriate for you, but I just read the (pause) a very thick biography on Alexander Hamilton.

Riffling through the pages of the American Revolution, you see nearly everything that's taking place in modern times—happening in reverse. You hear James Madison warning about the infinite and poorly defined "war on terror," saying: "No nation could preserve its freedom in the midst of continual warfare."

You hear Thomas Jefferson warning against the growing power of the executive branch and its puppet, the Republican Party, saying: "Our country is now taking so steady a course as to show by what road it will pass to destruction, to wit: by consolidation [of power] first, and then corruption, its necessary consequence."

And you hear Tom Paine saying, "It is the duty of the patriot to protect his country from the government."

Can I get a witness?

In short you hear statesmen arguing about ideas, using power as a means to an ultimate end—the public good. And you see all the real core virtues of the progressive wing of the Democratic Party—or, as Howard Dean memorably put it, the Democratic wing of the Democratic Party—in full flower as they defeated the world's mightiest maritime empire.

The Enlightenment was the overarching philosophical support for the American Revolution, and the tyranny of the British Empire was the overarching provocation. But to really get into the nitty-gritty of why the Revolution resonates more relevantly now than ever, we've got to dig a little bit into the personalities of its architects and frontline fighters.

FOUNDING BADASSES

If you live in the United States, or any of its "holdings," it's impossible to escape the Founding Fathers. One of them is on the crumpled-up dollar bill you just pulled out of your back pocket after doing the laundry. Another one is staring sternly down the avenue from his perch above a traffic circle. Your office building bears another one's name. The street you live on is named after yet another. If it's semipermanent and if it's "official," then it's probably named after one of the heroes of the American Revolution or the Constitutional Convention.

But there's something imaginary about these guys, something not quite real. They aren't men as much as they are myths. Despite the spate of Founder biographies that have been published in the last five years, few people, besides political science majors and law students, really know who these fellows actually were. Abstractions at best, total ciphers at worst. And yet they are the most important American citizens who ever lived, Americans before there even was an America. And they became that way because they were hard men. They were street fighters in fine wigs. They were outlaws with the finest minds this side of the Atlantic. They were considered "terrorists" by the British, ripe for a hanging if British forces captured them during the Revolution. Some of them had extramarital lady friends. Others could drink anybody under the table. Still others had hair-trigger tempers.

They were not tepid. They were not indecisive. They were not rarefied. And they were anything but boring. Because they will be appearing and reappearing throughout this book, it is useful to know exactly who we're dealing with.

By reexamining the lives and ideals of the men who founded this country, and designed its government, we can better assess where we are politically, at present, where we *should* be, and where we *can* be.

There are hundreds of excellent resources for information on the lives of the Founders (a selected list can be found in the back of the book). This book does not offer detailed biographies of the Founders; instead, in the pages that follow, the acts and words of the men profiled below will be expanded upon and compared with those of our current political leaders. For now, let's briefly get reacquainted with the men who made America.

YE OLDE CATALOGUE OF WHOOP-ASS

GEORGE WASHINGTON (1732–1799)

BACKGROUND: Virginia landowner.

KNOWN FOR: Being the first president, being illustrated on low-denomination currency, chopping down a cherry tree, not lying about it, having a capital named after him.

SHOULD ACTUALLY BE KNOWN FOR: Straddling the camps of radicals and pragmatists, Southerners and Northerners, landowners and merchants, and uniting the thirteen bickering American colonies at the time when no one else could accomplish the feat. Oh, and that cherry tree thing? Never happened.

ULTIMATE BADASS MOMENT: Overlooking, for a moment, all the times Washington survived death in battle, we should turn our eyes to the political world. After the defeat of the British Empire, Washington was in a position to become the unrivaled and unchecked monarch of the newly ascendant American States.

He turned it down.

WHO KNEW? In 1781, he wrote an angry letter to the caretaker of his Mount Vernon estate after "refreshments" were served to visiting British troops during the Revolutionary War. "It would have been a less painful circumstance to me," Washington wrote, "to have heard, that in consequence of your non-compliance with their request, they had burnt my House, and laid the Plantation in ruins."

QUOTABLE QUOTE: "I have ever thought religion a concern purely between our God and our consciences, for which we were accountable to Him, and not the priests."

ALEXANDER HAMILTON (1755–1804)

BACKGROUND: Orphan from the British West Indies.

KNOWN AS: "That hot guy on the ten-dollar bill."

KNOWN FOR: His unfortunate gunfight with Aaron Burr.

SHOULD BE KNOWN FOR: Co-creating the U.S. Constitution. Fighting parochial interests in order to obtain the federal assumption of state debt and the establishment of modern, British-style banking and credit systems. Writing most of the Federalist Papers under crazy deadlines. Founding the U.S. Treasury and designing the country's banking system. And being "that hot guy on the ten-dollar bill."

ULTIMATE BADASS MOMENT: In 1777, he rode on horseback from Philadelphia to Albany, New York, covering sixty miles a day for five consecutive days. His mission: to obtain desperately needed troops for General Washington from Commander Horatio Gates. That ride, along with others undertaken for similar reasons, damaged his health and almost killed him.

OR

Dueling with Aaron Burr because of a political disagreement. Your choice.

WHO KNEW? In 1791, while secretary of the treasury, Hamilton got entangled in the first really juicy national sex scandal. He made the mistake of sleeping with Maria Reynolds, a married woman whose husband, James, blackmailed him for money. When James Reynolds got caught up in another scheme that involved speculating on Revolutionary War veterans' unpaid wages, he tried to implicate Hamilton. Hamilton turned over to investigators his love letters to Maria, which exonerated him in the speculation scandal. Hamilton thus confessed the affair and denied any governmental wrongdoing, sacrificing his private reputation (as a faithful husband) to clear his public reputation (as treasury secretary).

QUOTABLE QUOTE: "The sacred rights of mankind are not to be rummaged for, among old parchments, or musty records. They are written, as with a sun beam in the whole volume of human nature, by the hand of the divinity itself; and can never be erased or obscured by mortal power."

THOMAS JEFFERSON (1743–1826)

BACKGROUND: Virginia landowner.

KNOWN FOR: Writing the Declaration of Independence, sleeping with one of his own slaves.

SHOULD BE KNOWN FOR: Not only writing the Declaration of Independence, but also agitating relentlessly for a Bill of Rights that would attach to the Constitution and guarantee the individual liberties of all (*cough,* male, nonslave, *cough*) Americans.

ULTIMATE BADASS MOMENT: After his election as president in 1801, political supporters—a group of Baptists in Danbury, Connecticut —implored him to declare a national day of religious fasting. He turned them down cold. Even though Washington had set the precedent for a U.S. president declaring a religious fast day, Jefferson refused, writing:

"Believing with you that religion is a matter which lies solely between man & his god, that he owes account to none other for his faith or his worship, that the legitimate powers of government reach actions only, and not opinions, I contemplate with sovereign reverence that act of the whole American people which declared that their legislature should make no law respecting an establishment of religion, or prohibiting the free exercise thereof, thus building a wall of separation between church and state."

WHO KNEW? During Jefferson's service as governor of Virginia, British troops were a constant menace, compounded by his own lack of interest in military affairs. In early January 1781, the British attacked Richmond, the new capital of Virginia. Jefferson fled the city.

On June 2 of the same year, Jefferson quit the governorship at the end of his term. Two days later, British troops raided Monticello and very nearly captured Jefferson, his entire family, and several guests. Jefferson ran away. Again. For years to come, political enemies would exaggerate the nature of his escape much to their own amusement. This may be the only thing Jefferson has in common with current politicians.

QUOTABLE QUOTE: "In questions of power, then, let no more be heard of confidence in man, but bind him down from mischief by the chains of the Constitution."

THOMAS PAINE (1737–1809)

BACKGROUND: Son of a poor British corset maker.

KNOWN FOR: Writing *Common Sense,* the pamphlet that helped spur the American Revolution, and the inspiring opening to "The Crisis": "These are the times that try men's souls . . ."

SHOULD BE KNOWN FOR: Giving the American Revolution its original throaty voice of courageous defiance and inspiring the Declaration of Independence, as well as writing articulately about the need for a wall of separation between church and state. Also, for adding to the fiery call for the legal defense of individual rights.

ULTIMATE BADASS MOMENT: While in France (in support of its radical revolution against the monarchy), Paine was imprisoned and almost beheaded. He escaped with his neck intact mostly because of a clerical error.

WHO KNEW? Much to his disappointment, Paine's fiery and uncompromising radicalism was muted and contained within the new American system, which preserved much of the substantial legal precedent of the British Empire. He died in New York in 1809, after years spent depressed, drunk, and diseased.

QUOTABLE QUOTE: "Not all the treasures of the world, so far as I believe, could have induced me to support an offensive war, for I think it murder."

BENJAMIN FRANKLIN (1706–1790)

BACKGROUND: Son of a Boston candle maker.

KNOWN FOR: Flying a kite, having bifocals, pioneering the modern art of celebrity self-promotion.

SHOULD BE KNOWN FOR: So completely charming the pants off the French elites that they intervened—with incredibly positive results—in America's favor during the Revolutionary War. Franklin's diplomacy was so influential that in the wake of Britain's defeat he was, after George Washington, celebrated as the most important leader of the Revolutionary War effort.

ULTIMATE BADASS MOMENT: Mercilessly satirized the British Empire with two biting pieces: "Rules by Which a Great Empire May Be

Reduced to a Small One" and "An Edict by the King of Prussia." These were published in 1773—when the British Empire was still very much a force to be feared. He wrote to his sister that his essays "held up a Looking-Glass in which some Ministers may see their ugly Faces, & the Nation its injustice."

WHO KNEW? As noted in his autobiography, Franklin courageously engaged in "intrigues with low women" and eluded "distemper."

QUOTABLE QUOTE: "Democracy is two wolves and a lamb voting on what to have for lunch. Liberty is a well-armed lamb contesting the vote."

JOHN ADAMS (1735–1826)

BACKGROUND: A Harvard grad and lawyer from relatively humble Braintree, Massachusetts, roots.

KNOWN FOR: Being the first vice president and second president of the United States, and thus a popular *Jeopardy!* response.

SHOULD BE KNOWN FOR: His fierce but collegial rivalry with Thomas Jefferson, which helped establish a crucial legitimate political dialogue about the strength of government that continues to this day.

ULTIMATE BADASS MOMENT: After the Boston Massacre of five colonists by British soldiers in 1770, several British soldiers were arrested and charged with the murder. Although already active in the Patriot cause, Adams nevertheless joined Josiah Quincy II in de-

fending them, winning them reduced sentences. Adams's courageous adoption of the unpopular side in this case resulted in his
subsequent election to the Massachusetts House of Representatives.
Adams's representation of the soldiers was the hallmark of his own
(and the Founding Fathers') style—the willingness to take an unpopular stand for the good of society as a whole.

WHO KNEW? John Adams and Thomas Jefferson died in separate
states on the same day, July 4, 1826—the fiftieth anniversary of the
signing of the Declaration of Independence.

QUOTABLE QUOTE: "Nothing is more dreaded than the national government meddling with religion."

JAMES MADISON (1751–1836)

BACKGROUND: Virginia landowner.

KNOWN FOR: Being the "Father of the Constitution."

SHOULD BE KNOWN FOR: Leading the effort to frame the Constitution.
Along with Alexander Hamilton, cowriting the enormously
thoughtful and revelatory Federalist Papers. Also drafted the
American Bill of Rights, which was based upon George Mason's
earlier work, the Virginia Declaration of Rights.

ULTIMATE BADASS MOMENT: Being an intellectual rock star and a crafty
political thinker. Madison maneuvered his vision for a federally
strong Constitution between the rocky reefs of geographic and

economic differences that divided the states (admittedly, this lacks some of the sex appeal of being gunned down by a sitting vice president).

WHO KNEW? The writer Washington Irving memorably sized up the pale, shy, unhealthy Madison: "a withered little apple-John."

QUOTABLE QUOTE: "A popular Government, without popular information, or the means of acquiring it, is but a Prologue to a Farce or a Tragedy; or, perhaps both. Knowledge will forever govern ignorance: And a people who mean to be their own Governors, must arm themselves with the power which knowledge gives."

To highlight the contrast between today's political leaders and America's founders, I've taken the liberty of updating and adapting an actual dispatch about General Washington's conduct during the Battle of Princeton to fit our current straits.

SIGHTING: NOVEMBER 8, 2004
Fallujah, Iraq

The Florida National Guard has just broken in the face of heavy machine gun and mortar fire. Suddenly, George W. Bush appears among them, urging them to rally and form a line behind him. A detachment of Marines joins the line, which first holds and then begins to move forward with Bush front and center, driving an armored Humvee. The Iraqi insurgents are placed behind a line of debris at the crest of a hill. Within fifty yards bullets begin to whistle and men in the front of the American line begin to drop. At thirty yards Bush orders a halt and both sides open fire simultaneously. An aide, Colonel Edward Fitzgerald, covers his face with his helmet, certain that his commander, so conspicuous a target, was cut down. But while men on both sides of him have fallen, Bush remains within his Humvee, untouched. He turns toward Fitzgerald, puts his hand on the colonel's shoulder, and says: "Away, my dear Colonel, and bring up the troops. The day is ours." And it was.

The closest actual modern equivalent is the proud displaying of a prop Thanksgiving turkey in the middle of a heavily defended military base far from the actual fighting.

You can, of course, make the argument that in modern times, the U.S. president would never need to serve on the front lines in the same way that Washington did. The flip side of that realistic assessment is that in colonial times, George W. Bush and friends would have almost certainly been pro-British merchants making a killing selling whale oil to the Hessians.

A REVOLUTION TO DIE FOR

Popular perception of the American Revolution has turned the event into equal parts folk kitsch (as anyone who has been pitched a low-cost dinette set by a George Washington look-alike can attest to) and soft-focus military-romantic garbage. It's become enough of a blank slate that its principles can (and have) been invoked by proponents of every manner of law or policy, in complete disregard of the original nature of the Revolution itself.

But there was no such blurriness at the time. The progressive principles for which the revolutionaries would fight and die were clear and vivid then, when "tyrannical" accurately described the day-to-day enemy and wasn't just a cool adjective to be used in the execution of Machiavellian foreign policy.

In order to pull some of the moss off those principles, let's step back and take a look at the nature of the American Revolution itself.

On the night of December 16, 1773, three merchant ships—the *Dartmouth,* the *Eleanor,* and the *Beaver*—sat moored at Griffin's Wharf in the port of Boston. Surging toward them through a crowd of colonial supporters were three raiding parties of American colonists dressed as Mohawk Indians.

Before thousands of silent onlookers, the groups fanned out onto the ships wielding axes and hatchets. Led by a revolutionary firebrand named Samuel Adams, the demonstrators, with an unflustered efficiency that would make Martha Stewart proud, trashed 342 crates of British tea, dumping the precious cargo into the harbor.

The whole thing had started over money. The American colonists were being taxed, and taxed hard, by the British. The British felt the colonists owed the Crown for the soldiers who kept the Indians at bay; as a result, a series of oppressive tariffs were set into place: The Molasses Act. The Sugar Act. The Stamp Act. The Townshend Act (collecting duties on glass, lead, paint, tea, and other odds and ends). The list went on and on.

The American colonists weren't interested in paying taxes on everything from paper to maple syrup, and they howled in protest. The day's battle cry was "No taxation without representation." When the Tea Act was passed in British Parliament in 1773, tension exploded into confrontation. The East India Tea Company had run into financial difficulty, and British government decided that a tea tax on tea shipments coming into colony ports was just what the doctor ordered. The colonists responded by boycotting tea.

Although it seems a harmless and perhaps painless protest, tea was a little bit like oil in those days. It was by far the most important product Britain sent from its ports, and in the colonies, it was a vitally important good. Everyday life could grind to a halt without it. (Imagine the entire country boycotting oil and gas when the prices rose outrageously during Hurricane Katrina.) The tea boycott was the first instance of mass mobilization in the nascent country—the first major protest of government policy. Acting collectively, various colonies consulted about ways to keep East India Company from entering their ports with their tea cargo. Outside Boston, East India Company agents were "persuaded" to quit their posts. Shipments of tea were returned to sender, or even put into storage.

But in Boston, a party was in the making. East India agents refused to resign. Incoming ships bearing East India cargo made plans to make port, despite colonial protests. That was a grave mistake. As news of the Boston Tea Party hit the streets, other port cities began hosting their own tea parties, and it was on.

Although the Brits considered this an act of terrorism, it was hardly that. After dumping the tea cargo, the colonists removed their shoes and swept the decks of the ships they'd just raided. They insisted that each ship's first mate verify that the Sons of Liberty had destroyed only the tea on board, and committed no other acts of destruction. This wasn't a riot or a mob. This act of protest was the carefully planned conclusion to a campaign against British favoritism of its own merchants at the expense of colonials.

The tension over military abuses and taxation without representation had been simmering for years, and the Boston Tea Party outraged the British. They responded with a series of draconian measures (known as the "Intolerable" or "Coercive" Acts) that would pour gasoline on the already hot flames of rebellion. These four acts of British Parliament closed the port of Boston, curtailed the powers of self-government in the colony, allowed British officers to be tried in other colonies or in England, and allowed the quartering of troops in the colonists' barns and empty houses.

Within two years, the symbolic drama of the Boston Tea Party, which, despite the whimsical name, was an act of profound subversion, would flare up into a full-force revolutionary uprising against the British occupation. The progressive forces of the American Enlightenment would harness years of anger stoked by economic and military oppression and turn it into a transformative tidal wave that would radically change the world.

Two Revolutions

In the 1770s there were, in fact, two American revolutions taking place. Inextricably linked, both were critical to creating the America we currently know, love, sometimes protest, and always worry about.

The first revolution consists of the physical acts that brought about American independence. It's best described as a series of pitched skirmishes, long retreats, and grinding irregular warfare that dragged on for seven brutal years. This is the revolution that's most often discussed: farmers and blacksmiths pluckily fending off some of the best trained and armed troops in the world with a combination of tenacity and courage. Lexington. Concord. Bunker Hill. Germantown. Valley Forge. Their very names strike fear in the hearts of fifth-grade field-trippers throughout New England.

Then there's the inspired military leadership by General Washington, a triumphant victory, and the overthrowing of Evil by Good. Cue fireworks and martial music, and would anyone like another burger before I shut the grill down for the night?

But the story of the first revolution misses the point. Simmering anger over economic issues was a critical catalyst for the changes that would transform America, and the military battles that ensued were vitally important. But to say that the revolution was nothing but a bunch of pissed-off peasant warriors who'd had enough taxes and thought "freedom" was better than "tyranny" misses most of the really good stuff.

Indeed, hundreds of other revolutions have been fought against tyrants throughout history, under similar circumstances; the wave of African and Asian revolutions against colonial masters in the mid–twentieth century, for example. But few, if any, had the same kind of success as the American Revolution in terms of setting up a stable framework for a thriving postcolonial state.

It's the second revolution—which unfolded inside and beyond the revolution of guns and forced marches—that would be key to the American success story. It was a revolution of ideas, a fundamental shift in principles that the Enlightenment thinkers of the Revolution unleashed upon America and the world. Drawing from philosophers such as John Locke, Montesquieu, and David Hume, the Founding Fathers envisioned a country where government was accountable to the people—not the other way around. It may be difficult to envision these days, but this was a radical departure from the governing philosophies of most countries on earth at the time. Throughout most of the world, it went without saying that kings, tyrants, and other assorted rulers-by-might-or-birth ruled over vast populations, and that this was the correct way. Indeed, many believed it was the only way. The common folks were too ill informed, careless, lazy, stupid, etc., to govern for themselves. Leave it to the pale-skinned aristocrats to make things functional.

Coming out of this milieu, Enlightenment thinkers, like Hume and Locke, were way off-center. And their writings inspired a bunch of other off-center men.

War was an evil to be avoided at all costs, not the patriotic duty of an ambitious empire.

Free speech was something to be protected, even—and especially—when it was most offensive.

Government was a gathering of the people's representatives, open to the people's inspection, and checked by its own internal inertia and oversight.

They saw the overlap of church and state as a recipe for tyranny and a threat to the safety of true religious freedom.

They believed a strong police state was a threat to individual liberties, and they generally preferred to let some evil go unpunished than to punish innocent people by overzealousness.

And—perhaps most critically—they viewed the executive branch as a part of government that necessarily had to be restrained, hobbled, and answerable to Congress. There would be no monarchs on this side of the Atlantic.

In one awesome convulsion of argument, thought, writing, violence, and rebuilding, men like Washington, Adams, Madison, Jefferson, Franklin, Hamilton, and Paine created what Lincoln would later call "the last best hope on earth."

But close inspection of the historical record of the American Revolution reveals that nearly every progressive founding principle of that revolution has come under assault in recent years—by its own government.

War is no longer evil; it is a necessity, to be waged eternally against poorly defined enemies and at the convenience of the majority party.

Free speech is something that has "limits" (as does freedom, according to George W. Bush).

"Checks and balances" has become a joke as federal agencies have been neutered by the appointment of political hacks and loyal lapdogs. Congressional oversight and ethics committees have become rubber-stamp machines for the executive branch.

"Church" has become just another convenient way for the modern conservative movement to raise money, win elections, and demonize opponents, health of the "state" be damned.

The police state has become our friend, the supercharged "protector" that secretly snoops through our library records and homes at will, clutching the pernicious "PATRIOT Act" in its collective hand.

And the executive branch stands unchecked by either Republicans or, more troubling, Democrats. A steroid-crazed monster (with its Republican Party pusher), the Office of President draws strength from a cloud of fear kicked up by a never-ending war on terror and a seemingly never-ending war in Iraq.

The Founding Fathers knew firsthand the danger posed by an out-of-control executive with no respect for individual rights and representation. Another George with royal ambitions personally represented the antithesis of the Founders' Enlightenment vision for a transparent, accountable republic: King George III, a man adept in the ways of patronage and bribery.

Slow down the ship of state, the Founders advised, cut its sails and make the wheel hard to turn—but don't burn up the vessel, and don't sink it. Many of the Founders (Washington, Adams, Hamilton, at any rate) wanted a strong federal government, but all of them wanted that government to be accountable and supervised—a rare thing in the world then, and now.

After so much painstaking, brilliant, and courageous work to design an apparatus as close to perfect as the original American democracy, then, it's almost painful to watch the Bush administration try to take it apart. Nearly every move made by the Bush administration seems like an attempt to take the hobbles off and get the ship of state moving as quickly as possible—damn the consequences.

More government documents have been classified than ever before. The increasingly powerful hand of the executive branch has paved the way for war and torture by using that modern magic fairy dust—fear. The "nuclear option"—changing Senate rules to eliminate the filibuster—has not yet been invoked, but has so often been dragged into the public debate that its invocation can be seen as legitimate. Traditionalists who hearken back to the progressive virtues of the Founders have seen a running five-year assault on the most basic values.

It's time to examine and debunk conservative claims that tie the right-wing political agenda to the visionary ideas of America's founders—one PATRIOT Act at a time.

THE Alternate Universe DAILY SPECTATOR

SEPTEMBER 16, 2001

Bush: Protecting Liberties Comes First

WASHINGTON, D.C.—Five days after the most damaging domestic terror strike in American history, President George Bush is confounding critics who have called for the rapid passage of a so-called P.A.T.R.I.O.T. Act to strengthen the powers of law enforcement and intelligence agencies.

"We need to be vigilant in pursuing and apprehending the evildoers," Bush said at a press event in Washington, D.C., yesterday. "But we must not overlook the potential that exists to forever damage our precious civil liberties."

While conceding that the devastating attacks on New York and Washington had "shaken our spirit," Bush added that while he was president, he would ensure that they would "never harm the fundamental liberties and protections of law that make this country great.

"I would be betraying my own conservative principles and the faith of the American people if I used this attack as an excuse to take away American liberties. Our law enforcement and intelligence agencies will do all they can to find the terrorists behind this attack, and any future attacks, and bring them to justice. But we will not take away the protections of the Constitution and our laws until we have had time for a true debate—a national debate, in the open—about what we need to do to respond to this assault."

Bush cited the example of America's first president, George Washington, in his call for caution on changing laws that might restrict the freedom of Americans.

"You all remember what George Washington said about letting 'angry and malignant' passions dominate a discussion instead of reasoned debate, don't you? We're not going to let that happen. If we pass a new security act in the wake of 9/11, it's going to be one that all Americans have time to read about and think about, because this changes the way we all live from here on in."

Closing his press conference, Bush invoked another Founding Father, Benjamin Franklin. "It was our most rotund and enlightened Founding Father, Ben Franklin, who wrote the immortal words: 'Those who would give up essential liberty to purchase a little temporary safety, deserve neither liberty nor safety.' I stand before you today ready to fight for those words, and protect tomorrow's legacy of freedom against the fear and anger of today."

TWO

PATRIOTS AND
THE USA PATRIOT ACT

It is seldom that liberty of any kind is lost all at once.
—David Hume

*Those who would give up Essential Liberty to purchase a
little Temporary Safety, deserve neither Liberty nor Safety.*
—attributed to Ben Franklin, 1759

IF, IN THE MONTHS following the 9/11 attacks, you asked many Americans about the erosion of civil liberties in the name of national security, you may have heard this classic explanation: "Only those with bad intentions need to be worried about the loss of civil liberties."

Like the philosophy of Jean-Jacques Rousseau, this posits a very positive view of government. It credits the government with honest decision-making and responsible use of its powers.

But America wasn't founded on Rousseau; it was founded on the ideas of philosophers who, while sharing Rousseau's love of freedom, designed their ideal governments on an assumption that people were a trail mix of greed, good intentions, incompetence, idealism, self-interest, and other traits. There was, they believed, no single "general will" that a strong government could promote and respect without legitimate opposition. Somebody was always going to be pissed off about something.

Thomas Jefferson spent most of his life obsessed with the many ways a government could erode the liberty of its citizens. He wrote endlessly on the topic and, as a result, has become the patron saint of those who fear an overreaching federal government. On the Constitution, for example, Jefferson wrote that "the absence of express declarations ensuring freedom of religion, freedom of the press, freedom of the person under the interrupted protection of the Habeas corpus & trial by jury in civil as well as in criminal cases excited my jealousy."[2]

It wasn't enough that the Constitution implicitly protected individual rights by not explicitly claiming domain over them. Jefferson knew that implicitness was the better part of getting something like the PATRIOT Act passed. He wanted—and eventually got—a series of amendments to the Constitution that would explicitly outline the limits of government. These amendments became, of course, our Bill of Rights. The original ten amendments are reproduced in their entirety below:

THE BILL OF RIGHTS
Amendments 1–10 of the Constitution

The Conventions of a number of the States having, at the time of adopting the Constitution, expressed a desire, in order to prevent misconstruction or abuse of its powers, that further declaratory and restrictive clauses should be added, and as extending the ground of public confidence in the Government will best insure the beneficent ends of its institution;

Resolved, by the Senate and House of Representatives of the United States of America, in Congress assembled, two-thirds of both Houses concurring, that the following articles be proposed to the Legislatures of the several States, as amendments to the Constitution of the United States; all or any of which articles, when ratified by three-fourths of the said Legislatures, to be valid to all intents and purposes as part of the said Constitution, namely:

AMENDMENT I

Congress shall make no law respecting an establishment of religion, or prohibiting the free exercise thereof; or abridging the freedom of speech, or of the press; or the right of the people peaceably to assemble, and to petition the government for a redress of grievances.

AMENDMENT II

A well-regulated militia, being necessary to the security of a free state, the right of the people to keep and bear arms, shall not be infringed.

AMENDMENT III

No soldier shall, in time of peace be quartered in any house, without the consent of the owner, nor in time of war, but in a manner to be prescribed by law.

AMENDMENT IV

The right of the people to be secure in their persons, houses, papers, and effects, against unreasonable searches and seizures, shall not be violated, and no warrants shall issue, but upon probable cause, supported by oath or affirmation, and particularly describing the place to be searched, and the persons or things to be seized.

AMENDMENT V

No person shall be held to answer for a capital, or otherwise infamous crime, unless on a presentment or indictment of a grand jury, except in cases arising in the land or naval forces, or in the militia, when in actual service in time of war or public danger; nor shall any person be subject for the same offense to be twice put in jeopardy of life or limb; nor shall be compelled in any criminal case to be a witness against himself, nor be deprived of life, liberty, or property, without due process of law; nor shall private property be taken for public use, without just compensation.

AMENDMENT VI

In all criminal prosecutions, the accused shall enjoy the right to a speedy and public trial, by an impartial jury of the state and district wherein the crime shall have been committed, which district shall have been previously as- certained by law, and to be informed of the nature and cause of the accusation; to be confronted with the witnesses against him; to have compulsory process for obtaining wit- nesses in his favor, and to have the assistance of counsel for his defense.

AMENDMENT VII

In suits at common law, where the value in controversy shall exceed twenty dollars, the right of trial by jury shall be preserved, and no fact tried by a jury, shall be otherwise re-examined in any court of the United States, than according to the rules of the common law.

AMENDMENT VIII

Excessive bail shall not be required, nor excessive fines imposed, nor cruel and unusual punishments inflicted.

AMENDMENT IX

The enumeration in the Constitution, of certain rights, shall not be construed to deny or disparage others retained by the people.

AMENDMENT X

The powers not delegated to the United States by the Constitution, nor prohibited by it to the states, are reserved to the states respectively, or to the people.

It's hardly surprising that the specter that continues to haunt the PATRIOT Act goes by the name Bill of Rights.

OF PATRIOTS AND POSERS

On August 30, 2004, nearly three years after the 9/11 attacks that marked the beginning of George W. Bush's "War on Terror,"

NBC's Matt Lauer asked the president if the "War on Terror" was winnable.

"I don't think you can win it," Bush replied. "But I think you can create conditions so that those who use terror as a tool are less acceptable in parts of the world."[3]

For the first time, the American public was told in plain terms what it had suspected: we were engaged in a poorly defined, unwinnable war against an indeterminate but sinister foreign enemy.

If James Madison had been sitting in the *Today* show greenroom, sipping bitter coffee from a styrofoam cup, he might have repeated something he'd written a couple hundred years earlier: "If tyranny and oppression come to this land, it will be in the guise of fighting a foreign enemy."

Yet if someone had taken Madison's words out of the steamer trunk of American history and into a national debate in the weeks following 9/11, he or she would have been torn apart. It is not inconceivable that an American citizen invoking these particular words would have been dismissed as an unpatriotic schlub.

In the moments after a stunningly vicious terrorist strike on a major American city, there was no room for a reasoned debate on American civil rights. Americans had very little patience for the ACLU during those post-9/11 weeks, even though the organization never strayed from its message. Nothing polarizes opinions like falling bodies and collapsing skyscrapers.

It was this fortuitous polarization that gave Bush and Company the green light to push the absurdly named PATRIOT Act. Without substantial public or private debate, without giving most legislators enough time to read through the hulking pile of paperwork that comprised the "Uniting and Strengthening America by

Providing Appropriate Tools Required to Intercept and Obstruct Terrorism Act of 2001," Bush signed the PATRIOT Act into law on October 26, 2001.

It was deeply discouraging to see the incredibly intense non-dogfight in Congress when this bill came up for vote. The mostly jingoistic debate in the U.S. House of Representatives—which in just about no way whatsoever resembled the passionate moments of the Constitutional Convention—led to a vote of 357 in favor of the passing the PATRIOT Act, to 66 opposed. In the (nominally) more deliberative Senate, the vote was even more lopsided: 98 to 1, with Mary Landrieu (D-LA) abstaining. Democrat Russ Feingold of Wisconsin was the only senator to vote against passing the PATRIOT Act, on principle.

Feingold's statement on the Act read, in part:

> . . . We must continue to respect our Constitution and protect our civil liberties in the wake of the attacks. As the chairman of the Constitution Subcommittee of the Judiciary Committee, I recognize that this is a different world with different technologies, different issues, and different threats. Yet we must examine every item that is proposed in response to these events to be sure we are not rewarding these terrorists and weakening ourselves by giving up the cherished freedoms that they seek to destroy. . . . We must also redouble our vigilance to preserve our values and the basic rights that make us who we are. The Founders who wrote our Constitution and Bill of Rights exercised that vigilance even though they had recently fought and won the Revolutionary War. They did not live in comfortable and

easy times of hypothetical enemies. They wrote a Con-
stitution of limited powers and an explicit Bill of Rights to
protect liberty in times of war, as well as in times of peace.

This was, at the time, crazy talk. It was considered by many to be treasonous. Feingold literally stood alone on the Senate floor on this vote, and many pundits predicted that Feingold's stand would doom his 2004 reelection campaign.

Instead, three years after the vote, Feingold triumphed by candidly explaining, in a series of campaign ads, his reasons for voting against the act. Wisconsinites respected the fact that Feingold kept it cool while ninety-eight of his colleagues were shitting fear-hardened bricks, and they reelected him.

But another reason Feingold won reelection was because in the intervening three years between the vote and the 2004 election season, American citizens had started to chafe under the restraints put into place by the PATRIOT Act. Widespread unease had become apparent—and it wasn't just the ACLU who was complaining.

People started wondering what, exactly, their elected representatives had passed when they voted yes to the PATRIOT Act. Some of those elected representatives were wondering the same thing; most had not even had the time to thoroughly read and vet, or have their staff thoroughly read and vet, the bill's contents, which was written mostly by current Secretary of Homeland Security Michael Chertoff and Assistant Attorney General Viet D. Dinh. If their elected representatives had no idea what exactly the PATRIOT Act was about, American citizens certainly didn't know what the score was, either.

But four years after its passage, little pockets of outrage began making noise across the country, as librarians, writers, journalists, and other Americans started to realize which of their rights had been signed away, without their permission. In fact, beginning in 2003, hundreds of communities across the country drafted official denouncements of the Act.*

Among the provisions in the PATRIOT Act that scared certain Americans:

- **Section 215:** The FBI may use this provision of the PATRIOT Act to obtain "any tangible thing," a category that includes letters, personal journals or diaries, library checkout records,† financial information, histories of your video rentals, membership lists of religious organizations, medical and psychiatric records, and—as the ACLU pointed out and former Attorney General John Ashcroft admitted in congressional testimony—genetic information.

- **Section 218:** An amendment to the existing Foreign Intelligence Surveillance Act, this section authorizes secret searches—authorized by a secret court. No one has to know what's going down, as long as the government simply alleges that it has a foreign intelligence basis for the search.

- **Section 213:** This provision gives the state the right to look through your stuff first, then tell you later. These

*Once the Department of Justice caught wind of these jitters, they launched a damage-control campaign. Then Attorney General John Ashcroft embarked on a bitchin' "Patriot Rocks" tour of nearly twenty cities, where he promoted the PATRIOT Act to dubious city officials.
†*Slate* termed the public outcry over Section 215 "the Attack of the Angry Librarians."

warrants allow for searches of your home without your prior notice—a 180 from the traditional obligation that the police let you know before they lay their hands on your stuff.

- Oh yeah—and wiretaps. Lots of 'em.

Fortunately, the courts, which typically use the Constitution and the Bill of Rights as their touchstone, have not been kind to the act over the years since its passage. In early 2004, a Los Angeles federal judge struck down Section 805 of the act (which classifies "expert advice or assistance" as material support to terrorism) because she considered it vague and in violation of the First and Fifth Amendments. U.S. District Judge Audrey Collins's decision was the first legal judgment to render part of the act unconstitutional.

In September 2004, U.S. District Judge Victor Marrero ruled Section 505—which allowed for the issuing of controversial "National Security Letters" to obtain customer records from Internet service providers and other businesses without judicial oversight—unconstitutional. It violated the First and Fourth Amendments. He also found the broad gag provision in the law to be an "unconstitutional prior restraint" on free speech.

As mentioned earlier, Section 215 allows judges to grant government investigators ex parte orders to examine personal phone and Internet records on the basis of being "relevant for an ongoing investigation concerning international terrorism or clandestine intelligence activities." But the Fourth Amendment demands "probable cause" in these cases, a much stricter standard.

Also known as the "library provision," Section 215 allows FBI agents to obtain a warrant from a secret federal court for the library or bookstore records of anyone connected to an investigation of international terrorism or spying. While under assaults in the courts and Congress, Section 215 still stands as of November 2005. A campaign to have this section "sunset," as originally planned, seems to have faltered and failed as the renewal of a full, if slightly tweaked, version of the act seems to be a fait accompli.

As if this sort of stuff—just a few of the croutons skimmed from a veritable salad of trampled rights—isn't unnerving enough, it's also unclear how many individuals or organizations have been charged or convicted under the PATRIOT Act. It'd be great to know, wouldn't it? Not going to happen: in keeping with the Bush administration's love of secrecy, the Justice Department refused to release that information throughout 2002 and 2003.

Even worse than the hidden abuses enabled by the PATRIOT Act are the hidden abuses that were enabled by nothing more than presidential hubris. The NSA eavesdropping scandal of late 2005 directly recalled the warrantless searching of colonial citizens that so riled Americans against their British masters—an arrogant executive branch intruding into the private sphere with a broad mandate and no checks on its power.

The NSA eavesdropping story finally popped into the public sphere when *The New York Times*—after an inexcusable year-long delay—decided to inform the public that Bush had personally authorized government spying on Americans without the obtaining of legal warrants.

The bypassing of Foreign Intelligence Surveillance Act courts betrayed a combination of laziness and arrogance shocking even to administration critics who were previously not shy about assigning huge boundaries to the expanse of the government's laziness and arrogance. FISA courts have approved more than 5,200 applications for warrants over the years; a whopping four have been rejected.[4]

FISA warrants can be obtained with a few hours' notice, and can even be obtained retroactively—in no way does following FISA guidelines constrain the government's ability to fight terrorism. It does, however, monitor and potentially prevent presidential abuse of power.

Attorney General Alberto Gonzales had the gall to suggest to Congress in January 2006 that NSA domestic eavesdropping was basically the same thing as George Washington's intercepting British military communications during the Revolutionary War. This misses a few crucial points, namely that Washington wasn't president during the war, he wasn't spying on American civilians, the Constitution didn't yet exist, FISA was more than two hundred years away, and—most pedantic—there weren't a lot of phone lines to tap in the eighteenth century. Or were there?

"President Washington, President Lincoln, President Wilson, President Roosevelt have all authorized electronic surveillance of the enemy on a far broader scale," Gonzales told Congress in February 2006.

Whether the NSA surveillance scandal blows up into a story with real legal implications remains an open question. A GOP Congress ensures that the lid will remain on; a transition of power and a watchdog Democratic Congress in 2006 could result in a more spectacular—and quintessentially American—check to the executive branch putting its ears and fingers where they don't belong.

A more combative Congress, spurred by the NSA, also embraced founding principles near the end of 2005 when it refused to authorize a long-term blank-check extension of the PATRIOT Act.

Opponents to the Act's extension were wise to note that they weren't against giving law enforcement more power to stop terrorism; they simply wanted the Act to be, uh, constitutional. Although a baby step in the big scheme of things, it's still a move in the right direction after a long forced march away from civil liberties as the Founders envisioned them.

But how did this hike into the woods of tyranny begin in the first place?

THE RIGHTS OF MAN

James Madison, apparently peering into the future with an extremely well-maintained and high-end-model crystal ball, wrote in his 1795 *Political Observations*: "No nation could preserve its freedom in the midst of continual warfare."

This concern for individual rights was endemic among the Founding Fathers, whether you're talking about Federalists such as Washington and Hamilton (who wanted an effective federal government, but took great pains to differentiate it from the tyranny of the British colonial system), anti-Federalists such as Patrick Henry, for whom local sovereignty and personal liberty was paramount, or radicals such as Tom Paine, who wrote in *Rights of Man*: "From the want of a Constitution in England to restrain and regulate the wild impulse of power, many of the laws are irrational and tyrannical, and the administration of them vague and problematical."[5]

In fact, it is Paine's words, perhaps more than those of the other Founders, that speak to the fundamental problem with the PATRIOT Act. It's a document intended to supersede the protections of the American people against their government, to override the Constitution's lawful protections (in terms of searches and seizures, and habeas corpus) against the tyranny of frightened or ambitious politicians.

It's the skeptical view of government—not necessarily cynical—that is most necessary when our liberty is on the line, the Founders believed. This belief stands in direct opposition to the "Patriot" shtick the Bush administration has been trotting out since 9/11. Patriots support their government unquestioningly, they'd have you believe. The more they shop, the more patriotic they are. They are willing to sacrifice small individual liberties in order to save their fellow citizens from another terrorist attack, even if the sacrifice of those liberties cannot be tied in any demonstrable way to effective antiterrorist activity.

The Founders would have us question during times of war, would have us prove our patriotism by participating civically rather than commercially, and would have us hold on to our civil liberties with extreme tenacity.

"It is easy to take liberty for granted, when you have never had it taken from you." These sage words are not from Thomas Jefferson, Benjamin Franklin, Abe Lincoln, Roosevelt, Kennedy, or any of the big guys. They are, instead, straight from Dick Cheney's lips to your ears.

As Cheney points out, we've largely lost our love of liberty, having enjoyed it for so long. We've become complacent.

Acutely aware of what it was like to live under the thumb of a powerful, nonrepresentative, unjust government, the Founding Fathers had a far more intimate understanding of the trade-offs between liberty and security. It's something Americans may have to relearn all over again.

SEPTEMBER 8, 2001

Bush Reveals Details of Secret Energy Meeting

WASHINGTON, D.C.—Putting the reputation of his own vice president at risk, President Bush yesterday made public the notes of a national energy-task-force meeting held in secret among industry leaders—with no environmental groups—near the beginning of the administration's tenure.

"Kings and dictators do their business in secret, not the democratically elected representatives of a free people," Bush said. "If there's one thing we learned from the American Revolution, it's that a free people need to be fully informed."

The newly revealed minutes of the meeting depict a transaction between the government and industry leaders that no one—not even the environmental movement's most outspoken members—could have predicted. A direct excerpt from the meeting follows:

VICE PRESIDENT CHENEY: Gentlemen, welcome. I understand that you're looking for us to weaken environmental protection laws so that you can increase drilling, boost profits, and compete more aggressively on the international stage. Your government hears you and . . .

EXXON REPRESENTATIVE: No, actually that's not it.

TEXACO REPRESENTATIVE: Yeah, that's not why we're here.

CHENEY: What? No?

EXXON: Not at all. We're here to secretly give 20 percent of our gross revenues back to the American people. We've got more money than we can use, frankly. . . .

CHEVRON REPRESENTATIVE: And we want to see the cash go to a good cause. We were thinking more park rangers. Reforestation. Protection for endangered species. That sort of thing.

CHENEY: What? Well, I guess I can see the PR value in a stunt like that. I can have my people put together a press release . . .

TEXACO: Ah, but that's just it. We don't want credit for it. We'd like it to be a secret mitzvah. Surely you've heard the old legend of the 36 Lamed Vav Tzadikim, or secret righteous men, whose good deeds keep the world from coming to end.

EXXON: That's how we see ourselves.

CHENEY: Of course. I understand completely. I'll do my best to make sure that this doesn't get out to the public. God bless you.

Phone calls to Vice President Cheney's office were not returned.

THREE

AMERICA'S INVISIBLE GOVERNMENT

A people who mean to be their own Governors, must arm themselves with the power which knowledge gives.

—James Madison

When you carefully consider FOIA requests and decide to withhold records, in whole or in part, you can be assured that the Department of Justice will defend your decisions.

—Former Attorney General John Ashcroft, October 12, 2001

THE POLEMICIST THOMAS PAINE (1737–1809) is one of the country's most challenging (read: pain in the ass) Founding Fathers, if he's numbered among that group at all. Of the Founders, he perhaps best symbolizes the spirit of outrage and rebellion—and best captures the fire of liberty that sparked the American Revolution. Provocative and irascible, Paine outraged as much as he inspired.

The son of a British corset maker, Paine spent most of his youth casting about, looking for a cause. He was twice fired from his job as an excise tax collector, being none too keen on extracting pennies from laborers. By chance he met Benjamin Franklin in London in 1774, and was persuaded to emigrate to Philadelphia. Among the first things he did in his adopted country, in addition to becoming editor of the *Pennsylvania Journal,* was to publish *African Slavery in America,* a searing critique of the institution of slavery in the United States.

As a former taxman, Paine also couldn't help but notice the rising discontent in the colonies over the increasing taxes Britain was extracting from its American subjects. He knew a break with Britain was inevitable.

> *I saw, or at least I thought I saw, a vast scene opening itself to the world in the affairs of America, and it appeared to me that unless the Americans changed the plan they were pursuing with respect to the government of England, and declared themselves independent, they would shut out the prospect that was then offering itself to mankind through their means.*[6]

Common Sense was published—anonymously—in 1776, and was an instant sensation. In no time, half a million copies were in circulation, a veritable Oprah's Book Club pick, colonial style. And it was, perhaps, the most important polemic ever written—a call to arms for revolution against the world's most powerful country, and an outline for a completely new brand of government.

Government, Paine wrote, was a necessary evil, an evil that could only be kept in check by a representative system that utilized regular elections. Government performed only regulatory functions, and was simple and spare. Republicanism is the only rational form of government, he wrote. Executive tyranny must be made impossible through the design of government.

But, he warned, "those who expect to reap the blessings of freedom must, like men, undergo the fatigues of supporting it."[7]

Paine actively agitated for revolution. The pages of *Common Sense* are filled with rhetoric so passionate, they are almost hot to the touch. Loyalists? Idiots, Paine said. The English Constitution? A sham. The British monarchy and hereditary succession? A tyrannical system headed by imbeciles.

A particularly Painesean moment occurs in the section titled "Of Monarch and Hereditary Succession":

> *To the evil of monarchy we have added that of hereditary succession; and as the first is a degradation and lessening of ourselves, so the second, claimed as a matter of right, is an insult and imposition on posterity. For all men being originally equals, no one by birth could have a right to set up his own family in perpetual preference to all others for ever, and tho' himself might deserve some decent degree of honours of his contemporaries, yet his descendants might be far too unworthy to inherit them. One of the strongest natural proofs of the folly of hereditary right in Kings, is that nature disapproves it, otherwise she would not so frequently turn it into ridicule, by giving mankind an ASS FOR A LION.*

A British subject calling his monarch an ass—in print—was a remarkable risk, and as incendiary a comment as was possible in those fractious times.

After *Common Sense* was published, the proverbial shit hit the fan. Loyalists hated him and grudge-bearing colonists made him an icon. Paine didn't merely talk about freedom of speech—he lived it. And that this sort of writer had a Founder fan club so attentive to the details of his ideology that one could say Paine had such a direct hand in shaping the Revolution's ideals, says a lot about the progressive tendencies of the leaders of early America.

In fact, Paine's December 1776 follow-up, *The Crisis,* was ordered by George Washington to be read to every revolutionary regiment in the colonies by their generals. Many historians attribute the victory at the Battle of Trenton to the passion the tract inspired in the American soldiers who triumphed in New Jersey that day. Its stirring opening ("These are the times that try men's souls") has passed from history into the fuzzy zone that lies between legend and cliché.

Bringing Paine's ideology into the current political dialogue presents a few problems. Paine wrote his most blistering tracts (*Common Sense, The Crisis*) during the conflict with Great Britain—as such, they're aimed squarely at a tyrannical monarch, not an elected American president.

Paine also had a weakness for the glamour of revolution—he launched himself into the midst of the French Revolution, where only a clerical error prevented his head from being lopped off by the guillotine. Gravely ill, he was nursed back to health by the new American ambassador in Paris, future president James Monroe.

But revolutionary excesses aside, Paine's ideas drove the American Revolution in at least two vividly relevant ways.

POWER OF THE PRESS

As a relentless polemicist and pamphleteer, Paine used the power of the press to change people's minds, to engage citizens in public debate, and to challenge the power of a government run amok. Without *Common Sense,* Paine's call for a separation from Great Britain (by violence, if necessary), the Revolution might never have found the ideological footing it needed to become a reality.

THE DANGER OF SECRECY IN GOVERNMENT

A passionate opponent of tyranny, Paine understood the danger of a government that worked in secrecy, staffed with personally loyal and unaccountable henchmen. He explicitly warned of the threat of a hereditary government, and spelled out one of the implicit thrusts of the Revolution—that the American government must be of the people, and accountable to the people. In its day, this was a radical notion.

This isn't to say that the Founders had a perfect record on the issue of secrecy. The Constitutional Convention was a secret meeting (although it sprang more leaks than a post-iceberg *Titanic*). And although the deliberations of the House of Representatives have always been public, the deliberations of the Senate were virtually secret for the first five years of the body's existence.

But much more so than the royalist government against which they were rebelling, the Framers envisioned a government that was public and accountable. George Washington was exceedingly conscious of the importance of preserving access to documents so that future historians could tell the story of America's birth, warts and all. Here's Washington writing to William Gordon in 1783:

> *I can only repeat to you, that whenever Congress shall think proper to open the door of their Archives to you, (which can be best known, and with more propriety discovered through*

the Delegates of your own State), All my Records and
Papers shall be unfolded to your View, and I shall be happy
in your Company at Mt. Vernon, while you are taking such
Extracts from them, as you may find convenient. . . .

I am positive no History of the Revolution can be per-
fect if the Historiographer has not free access to that fund
of Information.[8]

But like so many other comparisons between the revolutionary
era and current politics, it's important not to try to parallel but instead to examine, in current context, the intent of the Founders, and
the direction in which they were moving the country. Under King
George III, most of the critical decisions about colonial public policy were made in royal secrecy, buffered by the Atlantic Ocean and
an imperial bureaucracy. It left a bad taste in the mouths of unruly
subjects itching to live Humesian principles in a political petri dish
across the Atlantic.

The American Revolution brought government—and the information that fed and shaped public policy—into the hands of
representatives from the thirteen original states. It moved public debate into government, and took public policy decisions out of the
hands of an all-powerful king and his ministers into the hands of a
geographically representative legislature and a fallible and term-
limited president and his sometimes squabbling cabinet.

Washington even wrote in 1790 about the need for C-SPAN:

It is to be lamented that the Editors of the several Gazettes
of the Union do not more generally & more connectedly
publish the debates in Congress on all great National ques-

*tions that affect different interests instead of stuffing their
papers with scurrility & malignant declamation.*[9]

When you explore the writings of Paine, Washington, Jefferson,
Franklin, and company, you find an interest in disseminating "the
facts," a clear, accurate record of words and deeds that can be used
as a starting point for honest political discussion and debate. There
is excitement about universities, newspapers, open archives, and
scientific journals. A reader of ten different newspapers, George
Washington suggested that newspapers and other publications
should be exempt from postage costs in order to speed the flow of
information. George W. Bush, of course, is a reader of (maybe) one
paper, relying on his cabinet to filter the news for him.

What you don't see in the writings of the Founders is anybody
advocating for a tight relationship between a partisan press organization and government, wherein the press can be used to set a political agenda, distract voters, and disseminate disinformation. In
fact, that sort of coziness would likely have been vomit-inducing to
Tom Paine.

Perhaps most interesting, though, is that Washington's suggestions for boosting the reach (and, by extension, power) of the press
came at a time when sensational, biased, sloppy, and sometimes
downright demagogic newspapers were all the rage. Character as-
sassination and partisan cranks dominated the press to an extent
that makes the *New York Post* look like *The Christian Science
Monitor*. And it was Washington himself who was often the victim
of press attacks, particularly during the unfortunate "Americans
getting their asses kicked" portion of the Revolutionary War, when
Washington was losing more battles than he was winning. He also

suffered its slings and arrows while tangling with the sometimes ruthless tag team of Madison and Jefferson.

Jefferson, another proponent of a free press, felt the sting of that press, but like Washington saw the value in an independent source of news. President Jefferson addressed the question in his Second Inaugural Address, in 1805:

> *During the course of administration, in order to disturb it, the artillery of the press has been leveled against us, charged with whatsoever its licentiousness could devise or dare. . . . They might, indeed, have been corrected by the wholesome punishments reserved and provided by the laws of the several States against falsehood and defamation; but public duties more urgent press on the time of public servants, and the offenders have therefore been left to find their punishment in the public indignation.*[10]

ALL THE PRESIDENT'S MEN (AND REPORTERS)

George W. Bush hates the press. This is perhaps the one open secret in the Bush administration. His biographer Bill Minutaglio told NPR's Brooke Gladstone that Bush has always been suspicious of the media, openly blaming them for his father's loss to Clinton in '92. George W. was known as a "loyalty-enforcer or . . . backroom media monitor . . . a guy who, if he had determined that some member of the media had slighted his father, would approach that member of the media and essentially [say], Hey, you're frozen."[11]

Bush approaches the press issue from a perspective different from the Founders'. On one hand, the Bush administration has actively used propaganda: video "newsreels" actually produced by government agencies;[12] newspaper columnists and other assorted "journalists" bribed to produce favorable press for the Bush White House;[13] government health websites purged of data relating to safe sex;[14] and so on.

The Government Accountability Office, one of the few remaining aggressive checks on executive branch power, has taken note of all these instances and publicly chastised the administration for its use of what the GAO has termed "illegal government propaganda."[15]

The Bush team even brought its talking-hand-puppet approach to media management over to Iraq. In early December 2005, *The New York Times* discovered that the U.S. military had been engaging in a multimillion-dollar covert campaign—to plant paid propaganda in Iraqi newspapers, propaganda masquerading as hard news. The campaign, run by a Washington-based PR firm, also paid monthly stipends to Iraqi journalists who were friendly to the U.S. position, according to military contractors and officials interviewed by *The New York Times.*[16]

While the concept of paid news may not be foreign to those who have lived under a dictatorship or even under Communism, for those living in a developing "democracy by force," Thomas Jefferson's mandate couldn't be more mangled.

And on the other hand, the administration has proven almost impervious to actual reporting of real-world events. Bush's response to a challenging press corps is to stonewall it at farcical "briefings," and to ignore the reporting that results from those briefings.

"I glance at the headlines just to kind of [get] a flavor of what's moving," Bush told Fox News in 2003. "I rarely read the stories."

In fact, in order for Bush to be convinced that Hurricane Katrina was worthy of his attention, his aides had to cobble together a "Greatest Hits of Katrina" DVD and force him to watch it between bike rides.[17]

Just because George Washington read ten newspapers a day and Bush "glances" at the headlines doesn't mean Bush is necessarily a worse man than Washington. What it does mean, though, is that that fundamental desire for knowledge about the country one is leading, about the world one is interacting with, about the plights of American citizens, and their successes—about the state of the union in general—is absent from the leadership style of George W. Bush. It was present in the leadership styles of the Founders. In fact, it was imperative to the leadership styles of the Founders. Excitement about new information has been replaced by dread of new information.

SCOTT McCLELLAN AND THE ART OF SCREWING THE PRESS

Scott McClellan has raised the art of hosing over the press (and by extension, the public) to a Dalíesque new plateau. While it's true that the buck once stopped with President Truman, McClellan is the equivalent of a psychotic hockey goalie, whose only job is to identify the buck, cover it in brown paper, and then bury it in a hole as far from the president as possible.

Here's McClellan on June 26, 2005, on opposition to John Bolton's nomination as ambassador to the UN:

Q: It's not just the Democratic leadership or members of the Democratic Party—it's members of the president's own party, some of [whom] are calling for him to withdraw the nomination. So is he going to heed those calls or not?

McCLELLAN: No, that's not correct. . . . It's a minority of Senate Democrats that are preventing this nomination from moving forward. It's very clear that he has—

Q: Senator Voinovich is a Republican.

And here's McClellan, during the same press conference, combating charges of abuse at the Guantánamo Bay holding facility in Cuba:

Q: On Guantánamo and Africa—President Bush's new friend, Bill Clinton, has said that Guantánamo needs to be cleaned up or closed. What are your thoughts about that, as you're saying that the allegations have been looked into?

McCLELLAN: Well, I'm not sure specifically what he's referring to.

Q: He's referring to the abuse and the problems at Guantánamo Bay.

McCLELLAN: And what abuse are you referring to?

Q: The abuse of the prisoners, the fact that the prisoners, some of them—you still have, what is it, five hundred—

McCLELLAN: So you can't point to anything specifically.

Either McClellan's being cute, or he actually hadn't read the accounts of a freed British prisoner, visiting FBI agents, veteran *New Yorker* investigative journalist Seymour Hersh, the Red Cross, Amnesty International, and the Pentagon itself, all of which pointed to incidents of torture.

Finally, here's McClellan on July 6, 2004:

McCLELLAN: Well, we have learned since going into Iraq and removing that regime from power that the regime certainly had the intent and capability when it comes to weapons of mass destruction.*

That's one way to phrase it, yes. Another way to phrase it is to say, "We found bubkes, but we're going to say 'intent and capability.' " McClellan's Waterloo moment came in July 2005, when new information about the leak of CIA agent Valerie Plame's identity prompted a White House clampdown on information regarding the investigation, and a sudden retreat from the president's pledge to fire anyone involved in the leak. The press was righteously infuriated, and they rose to the occasion, grilling the press secretary.

McClellan offered many memorable responses, but a sampling

---

*This is just a Whitman's Sampler of spin; every American citizen should read ten or twenty McClellan briefings and then, using a reputable news source, check his accuracy.

of his Top Ten might be the best way to express the spirit of the discussion:

SCOTT McCLELLAN'S TOP TEN

10. I DON'T THINK WE SHOULD BE PREJUDGING THE OUTCOME OF ANY INVESTIGATION AT THIS POINT.

9. WHILE THAT INVESTIGATION IS ONGOING, THE WHITE HOUSE IS NOT GOING TO COMMENT ON IT.

8. NO ONE WANTS TO GET TO THE BOTTOM OF IT MORE THAN THE PRESIDENT OF THE UNITED STATES.

7. I THINK THE WAY TO BE MOST HELPFUL IS TO NOT GET INTO COMMENTING ON IT.

6. I THINK WE'VE EXHAUSTED DISCUSSION ON THIS THE LAST COUPLE OF DAYS.

5. EVERYBODY IS GOING ABOUT DOING THEIR BUSINESS, AS THEY SHOULD BE.

4. I WILL BE GLAD TO TALK ABOUT IT AT THE APPROPRIATE TIME.

3. I'LL TRY TO COME BACK TO YOU IF I CAN.

2. YOU'VE HEARD MY RESPONSE ON THIS.

1. I APPRECIATE YOUR QUESTION.

Now, it's easy to be cynical about a press secretary whose main job—particularly during the buildup to the Iraq war, when the earnest ramming of "WMD," "Al Qaeda" and "Saddam Hussein" into public statements was job number one for the White House—seems to be preventing the American people from knowing what's actually going on. What else should a press secretary do but lie to the press and protect the president? What else can we expect? In a dictatorship we would expect nothing less. In fact, that's pretty much what TASS, the Soviet press agency, was tasked to do during the good old days of the USSR.

But despite appearances, McClellan's not the president's hireling. Like everyone else in government, he is a public servant, accountable to the public. Press secretaries aren't political consultants, and shouldn't be merely hot- and cold-running spin machines; they should be accountable in some way, shape, or form to the truth. It's shocking, but he is not paid to protect the president; he's paid to facilitate the press.

Who was George Washington's Scott McClellan? It was George Washington.

SECRECY IS THE SPICE OF LIFE

If the Bush administration had an official motto in regard to its opinion about the press, it would be: "How dare you—*how dare you*—ask us to divulge the information we're using to make public policy." A natural impulse toward control-freak governance has been compounded, of course, by the aura of "wartime" hysteria surrounding the post-9/11 era. Certain specific military and law enforcement secrets—the identity of CIA agents, for example—become vital information in times of war.

But secrecy* breeds scandals. Wherever the prying eyes of the public (and your political opponents) don't go, opportunities for graft, sabotage of the public good for ideological reasons, and good old-fashioned incompetent decision-making abound. Scandals are like cockroaches—if one stumbles out onto the kitchen floor while you're fixing yourself a sandwich, you can bet that it has five hundred pals cozily ensconced in the floorboards and insulation.

One of those cockroaches was the political background of the otherwise pleasant-seeming Harriet Miers, Bush's failed nominee for Supreme Court justice in 2005. In considering Miers for the position, Senate Democrats had a fairly simple request: "May we please, if it's it not too much trouble, examine the documents Ms. Miers wrote during her nearly six years of service in the White House so that we can make an informed decision on approving the nominee?"

Democrats wanted access to documents authored by a public employee serving in a public position so they could evaluate and then decide whether to promote that public employee to one of the most powerful and unaccountable public offices in the nation. They

---

*As a researcher for *The Al Franken Show,* I was tasked with interviewing guests before they appeared on air. Few conversations through the years have been as memorable as the forty-five-minute pre-interview I conducted with former Nixon counsel John Dean. Dean—who experienced Nixon's paranoid penchant for secrecy firsthand—spoke in detail and with much intensity about how the Bush administration has made the Nixon administration look as clean and open as a Quaker picnic. This may just be a personal take on things, but when a Nixon insider gets upset about the rising tide of executive-branch secrecy, it may be time to do something about it. Dean points out in *Worse Than Watergate* that Bush took note when leaks relating to the Iran-contra scandal harmed his father's vice presidency, and rumors of Bush Sr.'s infidelity troubled his term as president, setting a pattern of aversion to public scrutiny that has carried over through both of the younger Bush's terms as president.

were not asking for access to nuclear secrets, or the details of classified negotiations with Iraqi insurgents. They were asking for information that in any private corporation in the country would be made available to decision makers before making a promotion of this magnitude.

Utah senator Orrin Hatch expressed the Republican Party line on transparency on October 4, 2005:

> *I think that most of the information they are to have to get from her is going to come in the form of question and at the hearings, because there is no way that the White House is going to give privileged documents to the Senate. That is just what you call a ruse. My colleagues on the other side will do that every time.*[18]

Ah, yes. The classic "obtain information before making an important public policy decision" ruse that the Founders liked so well. The oldest trick in the book. Luckily Hatch is too smart for those kind of antics.

Into the gaping maw of organized silence, Senator Edward Kennedy attempted to put the rampant growth of secrecy in perspective in the summer of 2005 by reminding his colleagues that:

- The director of the government's Information Security Oversight Office, J. William Leonard, had publicly testified that "it is no secret that the government classifies too much information. Too much classification unnecessarily impedes effective information sharing."

- The deputy undersecretary of defense for counter-intelligence and security, Carol A. Haave, publicly stated that as much as half of all classified information *doesn't need to be classified.*

- In 2004, the Bush administration classified 15.6 million documents,* costing $7.2 billion, many under *newly invented categories* with fewer requirements for classification.[19]

But maybe that's just the way U.S. government works, right? Well, not exactly. Although the number of documents classified during the Clinton administration did represent an increase from prior administrations, Attorney General Janet Reno officially held that if a document could be released without causing harm, an agency should release that document. Even—and this is a critical difference between the MOs of the Clinton and Bush administrations—if there were technical grounds for withholding it.

Yet when the Bush administration came to office, claiming the originalist lineage of America's founders, Attorney General John Ashcroft quickly turned this crucial idea on its head. Ashcroft wrote that if there exists any technical ground for withholding a document under the Freedom of Information Act, an agency should withhold it. His now infamous October 12, 2001, memo instructed federal employees, in part:

---

*Actually, according to the Information Security Oversight Office, there were 15.6 million classification *decisions* made in 2004. One decision can cover multiple documents, so the number is probably much higher than 15.6 million.

When you carefully consider FOIA requests and decide to withhold records, in whole or in part, you can be assured that the Department of Justice will defend your decisions unless they lack a sound legal basis or present an unwarranted risk of adverse impact on the ability of other agencies to protect other important records.[20]

Less than a month later, Bush issued an executive order that seals all presidential records since 1980. All presidential records— public information—now unavailable to the public.

The cumulative effect of all this secrecy in government might lead a perceptive citizen to understand that the Bush administration is striving to become an invisible government—invisible, at least, to its own citizens: seen by no one, heard by no one, challenged by no one, impervious to criticism by the press and public, and protected by walls of silence and loyalty.

But, in some quarters, there are some people who, absurdly attached to the dusty old principles of the Founders, are taking issue with the right wing's invisibility strategy.

SUNLIGHT IS THE BEST DISINFECTANT

In 2005, Americans celebrated the first-ever "Sunshine Week," a celebration of all things Founder. Specifically, the week was meant to highlight the dangers the increasing secrecy surrounding the Bush administration poses to the ordinary American citizen.

"Any party in power is always reluctant to share information, out of an understandable—albeit ultimately unpersuasive—fear of arming its enemies and critics," wrote Senator John Cornyn

(R-TX) and Senator Patrick Leahy (D-VT) in a joint statement. "Whatever our differences may be on the various policy controversies of the day, we should all agree that those policy differences deserve as full and complete a debate before the American people as possible."

Together, Cornyn and Leahy are backing legislation that would create penalties for agencies that ignore FOIA requests. They have proposed a kind of ombudsman for FOIA—an independent arbiter—that would provide the public a way of appealing, in a more personal way, rejected requests.

When Leahy and Cornyn—a Democrat and a Republican—joined forces to push for more openness in Washington, some were surprised. Bipartisanship isn't exactly rampant inside the Beltway these days. But close examination of both progressive *and* conservative ideals reveals much common ground when it comes to the basic functioning of government. True conservatives believe in transparent government. Madison, Hamilton, Washington, and the rest of the crew believed that our government's legitimacy depended wholly on the trust of the citizens it governs. It was a radical idea—ultimately revolutionary—that stemmed from the desire for a government that did not operate in unseen quarters, making secret decisions and squirreling away documents in order that critics might be silenced.

The Founders didn't just expect dissent from the populace—they depended upon it. Without it, we were just another colony.

THE 𝔄lternate 𝔘niverse DAILY SPECTATOR

AUGUST 31, 2005

Despite Katrina's Wrath,
New Orleans Stays (Relatively) Dry

NEW ORLEANS—Two days after Hurricane Katrina's landfall on the Gulf Coast, homes are flooded, power lines are down, and most of coastal Louisiana and Mississippi is under a federal state of emergency. The storm has apparently taken dozens of lives up and down the coast. But the feared worst-case scenario of the New Orleans levees' failing has not come to pass.

Most experts are crediting the foresight of FEMA chief James Lee Witt and President George W. Bush for averting the disaster.

"Benjamin Franklin said, 'Never leave till tomorrow that which you can do today,'" said President Bush, surveying the scene at the presidential crisis center in Houston. "And that's what I believe in, too. FEMA has known for years that we'd need a few billion dollars to strengthen the levees around New Orleans because a catastrophic storm was one of the three most likely citywide disasters to strike the U.S. So I pushed Congress to put that money into the budget, and made sure it was spent wisely."

Mr. Witt, originally hired as FEMA director by former president Bill Clinton, was kept on in his post by President Bush. Bush noted the bipartisan praise that the capable disaster manager had received throughout his tenure.

"No need to fix something that isn't broken," said Mr. Bush in February of 2001, during the announcement of Mr. Witt's retention.

In completely unrelated news, former International Arabian Horse Association commissioner Michael Brown was found guilty of twelve counts of compound equine fraud relating to his mismanagement of the organization. According to a surprisingly strict interpretation of an 1821 cavalry statute, Mr. Brown was sentenced to be hung from "the old hickory tree."

FOUR

THE TIES THAT BLIND

In all our appointments of persons to fill domestic & foreign offices, let us be careful to select only such as are distinguished for morals and abilities. . . . We should seek to find the Men who are best qualified to fill Offices; but never give our consent to the creation of Offices to accommodate men.

—George Washington, draft of First Inaugural Address,
c. January 1789

Brownie, you're doing a heck of a job.

—George W. Bush, praising the work of FEMA director
Michael Brown after Hurricane Katrina, Mobile, Alabama,
September 2, 2005

I N GOVERNMENT, there are only two kinds of loyalty that really matter: loyalty to the public and loyalty to your political masters. Both kinds of loyalty have prices attached to them, but the exchange rate varies from administration to administration, and from post to post. In bad political weather, loyalty to the public can cost you promotions, respect, and even your job, as your unpopular and "disloyal" actions—meant to protect the American public and faithfully execute your duties—collide with the interests of your partisan leaders.

Lapdog loyalty, on the other hand, can win you praise, promotions, and protection—and/or an indictment, public embarrassment, and a career meltdown as you disgrace the office you hold in order to pursue personal gain and the promotion of your bosses' political agenda.

President Bush made it known that he is a big, pennant-waving, souvenir-hat-buying, foam-hand-wearing fan of lapdog loyalty. Many of his most prominent advisers and allies have been at his side since the early days in Texas; they do-or-die by the Bush team first and foremost.

There's nothing shocking about cronyism. It's as old as humanity itself, and no one wades into the scrum of politics without some good ol' boys on the team. The difference in modern years has been the embarrassing extent to which personal loyalty has supplanted professional experience at even the highest levels of government. They don't even try to hide it anymore.

The Bush administration, in particular, has been surprisingly adept at providing federal plums for loyal friends. Surprising because the Bush team ran on a "clean up Washington" platform during the 2000 election. Governors, not politicians, run the Bush ship.

Yet with Bush, under- or unqualified political appointees have risen to the top of federal agencies, and jobs that do not require Senate confirmation rose by almost 25 percent during Bush's first term.[21] The FDA's top lawyer between 2001 and 2004 was a Bush appointee not subject to Senate confirmation. That appointee—Daniel Troy—once worked on behalf of drug and tobacco companies. Previously the FDA position had been reserved for career officials with considerable experience.

"Normally, the chief counsel of the FDA is someone who comes up through the ranks," Representative Maurice Hinchey told the Bloomberg news service in September 2005. "[Troy] has a background of interests that are contrary to the interests he's supposed to have as chief counsel of the FDA. Essentially, the pharmaceutical industry was calling the shots."[22] Then there's Julie Myers, niece of former General of the Joint Chiefs of Staff Richard Myers. In September 2005, just days after the Michael Brown/FEMA meltdown, the United States Senate held a hearing to consider her qualifications. The Bush administration nominated her to head the U.S. Immigration and Customs Enforcement Agency, despite the fact that she had little immigration or customs experience. The agency, long the butt of Beltway jokes about its ineffectiveness, would operate under and report to the Department of Homeland Security, headed by Michael Chertoff.

Myers is married to Chertoff's chief of staff, John F. Wood.

"Though the White House attacked the diplomat Joseph Wilson for nepotism because he undertook a single pro bono intelligence mission while his wife was at the CIA," Frank Rich wrote in *The New York Times*, "it thought nothing of handing this huge job to a nepotistic twofer: Ms. Myers is the niece of Gen. Richard Myers and has just married [John F. Wood] the chief of staff for the homeland security secretary, Michael Chertoff. Her qualifications for running an agency with more than 20,000 employees and a $4 billion budget include serving as an associate counsel under Kenneth W. Starr; in that job, she helped mastermind the costly and doomed prosecution of Susan McDougal, and was outwitted at every turn by the defense lawyer Mark Geragos."[23]

And as deputy assistant secretary for money laundering and financial crimes at the Treasury Department, Myers was a top policy adviser on certain provisions of the PATRIOT Act.

In 1996, attorney Alberto Gonzales helped then Governor George W. Bush avoid jury duty in a drunken driving case. Why? Had Bush served on the jury, he would have had to disclose his own 1976 DUI arrest.

Less than ten years later, Bush named Alberto Gonzales the United States Attorney General.

The man in charge of saving the United States from toxic clouds and evil bird flu is a man named Stewart Simonson. He is, in the words of the the federal government, the man in charge of "the protection of the civilian populations from acts of bioterrorism and other public health emergencies."

Man, he must be the best of the best to be handling such important matters! And he is—if you're talking about the best of the best political lawyers. He has no experience in public health, in epidemics, or in bioterrorism. The former general counsel for Amtrak, he really knows his way around a commuter train. He's not quite so familiar when it comes to vaccines and all that other kind of disease-prevention stuff.

In defense of the Bush administration, this approach has been astoundingly effective in terms of "getting things done." But the Founders didn't design the federal government to "get things done" and create change simply at the behest of the current political leadership. Rather, they created a federal government that was accountable, checked and balanced. Moreover, they created a government that was answerable to and actually representative of the American people at large.

A faction-dominated government operating under absolute discipline and secrecy at the expense of public inquiry and accountability, in fact, would have reminded the Founders of the monarchal tyranny they strove to overthrow during the Revolution.

FOUNDER FOGEYISM

In 1790, Thomas Jefferson received a petition from his nephew, John Garland Jefferson, who hoped that his famous uncle could arrange for him a comfortable government job. Jefferson would have none of it.

His curt reply: "There is not, and has not been, a single vacant office at my disposal."[24] Instead, the Sage of Monticello sent his hapless relative a three-column reading list of books that would take two to three years to get through—and prepare him for a career as a lawyer.

In the Bush era, John Garland Jefferson would have been running FEMA.

George Washington was so concerned with merit, and so unconcerned with loyalty, that he put Thomas Jefferson in his first cabinet despite Jefferson's sometimes volatile disagreements with Washington and Hamilton, who was Washington's right-hand man and a principal architect of American government.

The Founding Fathers—both in and out of government—were men who often disagreed with one another about fundamental political principles. Key issues—the power of federal government, the independence of states, the role of the executive branch, postwar relations with Britain—divided them and sometimes set them at one another's throats.

But Washington, who valued the council of many voices, and listened carefully before setting his course, didn't see his role as that of a strongman, bending others to his will. He saw himself as a free man, elected temporarily to lead other free men. And with freedom comes free will, and free speech, which sparks argument, objections, debate, and internal divisions. The best way to get things done? No. The most reliable way to find the best ideas? Yes.

For Washington, the idea of issuing talking points and mandating the speech of his officials would have smacked of sinister royalism—and an inherently cynical distrust and abuse of the public will. "Liberty is to faction what air is to fire," wrote James Madison in the *Federalist No. 10*. You can snuff out disagreement, but only by smothering freedom itself.

These days, of course, the best way to get ahead is to refrain from asking inconvenient questions or objecting to flawed policy. The success of mouthpieces such as Scott McClellan and Karen Hughes, of ciphers such as Harriet Miers, and Mafia-style enforcers such as Tom DeLay and Karl Rove attest to the value and rewards of loyalty—and the willingness of the administration to use fear as a means of instituting it. Take the packing of the House Ethics Committee in order to save Tom DeLay's permanently endangered hide, for example. *The Washington Post* reported:

> *House Republican leaders tightened their control over the ethics committee yesterday by ousting its independent-minded chairman, appointing a replacement who is close to them and adding two new members who donated to the legal defense fund of House Majority Leader Tom DeLay (R-Tex.).*
>
> *Republican officials have spent months taking steps to ensure DeLay's political survival in case he is indicted by a*

*Texas grand jury investigating political fundraising, and
House leadership aides said they needed to have the ethics
committee controlled by lawmakers they can trust.*[25]

Fair-minded Republicans needed the ethics committee controlled
by lawmakers they could trust. This sort of naked partisanship and
lapdog loyalty would be embarrassing on any other legislative committee; but on the ethics committee, the action marinates and cooks
in its own self-satirizing juices.

Sacking Republican Representative Joel Hefley of Colorado because he wasn't loyal enough (loyalty in this case was measured by
a willingness to protect a now indicted corrupt member of
Congress) proves that the sword of loyalty cuts both ways. Not only
do hacks rise within the system and retain uncheckable power, good
civil servants pay for the choice to place ethics above personal loyalty with the destruction of their career.

Here's a whirlwind tour through just a few of the competent
civil servants sacked for putting the public interest over the political good of their leaders:

NAME: **Bunnatine ("Bunny") Greenhouse**
FORMER POSITION: Top official at the U.S. Army Corps of Engineers
in charge of awarding government contracts for the reconstruction of Iraq.
UNPOPULAR MORAL DECISION: Raised objections about secret, no-bid
contracts awarded to Kellogg Brown & Root (KBR)—a subsidiary of Halliburton.
QUOTABLE QUOTE: Described a particular Halliburton deal as "the
most blatant and improper contract abuse I have witnessed during the course of my professional career."[26]

NAME: Richard Clarke

FORMER POSITION: President Bush's chief adviser on terrorism on the National Security Council.

UNPOPULAR MORAL DECISION: Becoming disillusioned with the "terrible job" Bush and Company were doing against terrorism, and the spurious Al Qaeda–Iraq–WMD link.

QUOTABLE QUOTE: When Clarke wrote a memo explaining there was no Al Qaeda–Hussein link, it got bounced back to him with a note reading: "Wrong answer. Do it again."[27]

NAME: Paul O'Neill

FORMER POSITION: Secretary of the Treasury.

UNPOPULAR MORAL DECISION: Questioning the wisdom of massive tax cuts for the wealthy and the war on Iraq.

QUOTABLE QUOTE: "From the very beginning, there was a conviction, that Saddam Hussein was a bad person and that he needed to go."[28]

NAME: Lawrence Lindsey

FORMER POSITION: A top economic adviser to Bush.

UNPOPULAR MORAL DECISION: Revealing that a war with Iraq could cost $200 billion—which has turned out to be one of the administration's most honest predictions to date, if not a long-term lowball.

QUOTABLE QUOTE: During his 1991–1997 tenure at the Fed, Lindsey said, "It's the president's job to give us advice and it's our job to ignore it."[29] That worked under Clinton. It failed with Bush.

NAME: Rand Beers

FORMER POSITION: National Security Council's senior director for combating terrorism.

RESIGNED OVER: The war in Iraq being pursued instead of the war on terror.

QUOTABLE QUOTE: The administration "wasn't matching its deeds to its words in the war on terrorism. They're making us less secure, not more secure. . . . The longer I sat and watched, the more concerned I became, until I got up and walked out."[30]

These are just five examples picked from an orchard of qualified experts canned because they raised the public good in an inconvenient way. The list sprawls for pages, including numerous scientists, government conservationists, soldiers such as Anthony Zinni and Eric K. Shinseki, possibly Colin Powell, and career diplomats such as John Brown and John Brady Kiesling (both with more than twenty years of service under multiple presidents). While it's true that you need political discipline and cunning to achieve results in government—scholars of the administrations of Jimmy Carter and Lyndon Johnson can speak at length about what makes an effective or ineffective administration—it's also true that such ruthlessness needs to be in the service of some kind of agenda intended to help the public at large.

Hiring and firing an administration is one of the most critical jobs a president is tasked with. Having a team of smart, capable leaders with professional dedication to their jobs doesn't ensure a blazingly successful presidency—as often as not, they'll fight among themselves, and bog down the entire edifice of government in a series of internal feuds.

But it sure beats the alternative.

MICHAEL BROWN,
CRONY EXTRAORDINAIRE

Considering the dire circumstances that we have in New Orleans, virtually a city that has been destroyed, things are going relatively well.

Can I quit now?

Tie or not for tonight? Button-down blue shirt?

I am a fashion god.

Let me introduce to you Michael "Brownie" Brown, former director of the Federal Emergency Management Agency (FEMA). These bon mots, except for the first, which was uttered during a press conference, were offered via e-mail to various FEMA employees in the midst of the worst natural disaster in United States history: Hurricane Katrina.

By now, the story is very familiar. Brown, a former commissioner of judges and standards at the International Arabian Horse Association, was appointed to run FEMA in 2003, succeeding Joe Allbaugh (Bush's 2000 campaign manager).

Forty-eight hours before Hurricane Katrina made landfall, the airwaves had been choked with dire warnings, hyperbolic stand-ups by drenched reporters, and decades of general, and specific, concern about "the big one." The National Weather Service, usually tight-lipped and timid when it comes to proclaiming natural events "catastrophes" before the fact, warned of scenes of destruction on a scale that had never been seen before.

There were very few people in the United States, in the days leading up to Katrina, who were unaware that a massive hurricane was heading toward the Big Easy. Except for George W. Bush and Michael Brown and Michael Chertoff and Patrick Rhodes.

"I don't think anyone anticipated the breach of the levees," George W. Bush said days after the levees were breached, and decades after the first pleas from local scientists to fix a dangerously flawed levee system. In fact, in 2002, the New Orleans *Times-Picayune* published a five-part series on "The Big One" examining what might happen if a hurricane the size of Katrina hit New Orleans. The paper—with the help of scientists, hydrologists, engineers, climatologists, meteorologists, and other eminently qualified observers—predicted that two hundred thousand people or more would be unwilling or unable to evacuate the city. Thousands would die, the paper predicted, and those who did not would have to find shelter in the Superdome. City roads would become impassable, making aid next to impossible.

"I have not heard a report of thousands of people in the Convention Center who don't have food and water," Michael Chertoff, director of Homeland Security and overseer of FEMA, said as thousands of people in the Convention Center did not have food and water, scenes that were running twenty-four hours a day on CNN.

"Probably one of the most efficient and effective responses in the country's history," the deputy director of FEMA, Patrick Rhodes (formerly part of Bush's "advance" team), said of the federal government's response to Hurricane Katrina.

In an administration where political loyalty is the primary concern when vetting new hires, it's not enough to hire a nonpartisan or moderate expert. Nonpartisan experts "go public" when internal disasters are ignored. They talk to the press. They fight for the public good, sometimes against the political interest of the administration. They introduce dissent into an otherwise perfectly oiled machine.

Frank Rich wrote that after Michael Brown's forced resignation, the two top guns at FEMA who remained—one of whom was a local television reporter—"are not disaster relief specialists but experts in PR, which they'd practiced as advance men for various Bush campaigns. Thus *The Salt Lake Tribune* discovered a week after the hurricane that some one thousand firefighters from Utah and elsewhere were sent not to the Gulf Coast but to Atlanta, to be trained as 'community relations officers for FEMA' rather than used as emergency workers to rescue the dying in New Orleans. When fifty of them were finally dispatched to Louisiana, the paper reported, their first assignment was 'to stand beside President Bush' as he toured devastated areas."

The only safe hire is a political vassal, whose fortunes are tied up with the administration and the Republican Party. A "good soldier," in other words, who will always put the party before the people. A soldier like Michael Brown.

But under George Washington, a veritable civil war brewed in the cabinet, as Jefferson and Hamilton battled each other to make policy and define the direction of a new nation. They went at it hammer and tongs, and took it public when things didn't go their way. Jefferson, in particular, was skilled at quietly orchestrating attacks on Washington and Hamilton in the press—while he was a member of the administration.

True, Washington was often worn down by the hostility under

the federal roof. But he was determined to make his cabinet one that was composed of independent, fearless thinkers, not one that acted as an unquestioning unit. He simply put the smartest, most capable people in the positions where they could do the most good.

As the real world slowly intruded into Michael Brown's fantasy job, he began appearing on CNN and other news networks to explain himself. In an e-mail that was made public during the initial investigations of what went wrong in New Orleans, Brown's assistant gave him some sage advice:

"Please roll up the sleeves of your shirt, all shirts. Even the president rolled up his sleeves to just below the elbow. In this [crisis] and on TV, you just need to look more hardworking." And with those shirtsleeves rolled up, he looked so hardworking that he earned George W. Bush's praise: "You're doing a heck of a job, Brownie."

Faced with the gross incompetence of one of his commanders, Charles Lee, George Washington had him arrested and court-martialed.[31]

THE 𝔄lternate 𝔘niverse DAILY SPECTATOR

November 10, 2005

Bush Rebukes Kansas State Board of Ed.
Over Intelligent Design Ruling

WASHINGTON, D.C.—In a move that provoked rumbles of discontent from his fundamentalist base, President Bush today struck out at a Kansas decision to expand its state science education standards in order to allow "Intelligent Design" into its curriculum.

"I believe in God," said the president, "and I believe that He created the world. But I don't see why my religious beliefs belong in a science classroom, any more than one of those crazy religions where the Earth rides around on a turtle, or Odin the All-Father presides over an eternal battle in Valhalla, or some crazy Egyptian ram-god created the universe on a potter's wheel, or whatever." He added: "With all due respect."

Defending his statement to critics on the far right, the president cited the example of the Founding Fathers, who were controversially active in erecting a barrier between church and state. "All of those great guys—Washington, Jefferson, Adams—were concerned about mixing up religion and government. It's not because they hated religion. Not at all. It's because they loved religion, and knew that the best way to protect it is to keep it out of the dirt and mud of politics. And that's what I'm trying to do, too."

The president made a passionate argument that scientific consensus should be the only metric for public education. "America's scientists, engineers, and teachers are the backbone of its economic progress and dynamism. And anytime science loses, America loses."

According to educational standards in the other 49 states, theories taught to students must meet the scientific standard of "falsibility," a doctrine that the president explored during a rambling press conference that turned into something of a philosophical bull session.

"What's falsifiable? I'm glad you asked," said Bush. "Well, I talked to some scientists, and they put it into language that I could understand. 'Falsifiable' is like when my predecessor in this great office said, 'I did not have sexual relations with that woman.' That was falsifiable, as we all found out. Either he did, or he didn't. It could be tested. Now, of course, all that depends upon what your definition of 'is' is, but that's a whole 'nother question.

"Just funnin' ya, Bill," he added.

FIVE

IN INTELLIGENT DESIGN
WE TRUST

Our arguments will carry the day because the force and logic and wisdom of the Founders, all of them, are on our side.

—Karl Rove, November 10, 2005

An alliance or coalition between Government and religion cannot be too carefully guarded against. Every new and successful example therefore of a perfect separation between ecclesiastical and civil matters is of importance . . . religion and government will exist in greater purity, without (rather) than with the aid of government.

—James Madison, letter to Edward Livingston, 1822

IT'S NOT DIFFICULT to see why the terms "faith" and "faith-based" have become magic talismans in American politics. Public confidence in government has taken a series of body blows that started with Richard Nixon, carried through to the scandals and malaise of the Reagan and Bush I era, and blossomed into a national sex scandal of Clintonian proportions in the nineties. It's no wonder that many people have turned to the miracle cleaning solution that is religion.

Despite the bad rap it's gotten in recent years, religion brings us together for worship, for church picnics, for community service projects, for Bar Mitzvahs, for tedious but basically very nice wedding masses, etc. In short, at its best, religion creates a sense of community and honors ritual, providing a structure within which to celebrate the important events of our lives. Locally, socially, personally—it's very often a Very Good Thing.

But on the national level, it can be a Very Bad Thing. Pump millions (or billions) of dollars through its veins, and religion becomes a political animal, no more or less holy than any other venomous creature rooting through the economic leaf litter in a Hobbesian struggle to stay alive and grow stronger.

The Founders had lived this nightmare: a corrupt European religious establishment that sold salvation to the highest bidder and had its political rivals whacked. And they'd seen Puritans burning innocent people as witches, condemning "heretics," and snuffing out joy with Taliban-like passion.

"They would look with great horror upon a theocracy," says Brooks Simpson, a professor of history at Arizona State University. "In that sense, they'd be much different from their Puritan forebears who saw a much more intimate relationship between religion and statecraft."[32]

That horror was no abstract feeling, and a theocracy was not merely one of a hundred what-if scenarios. The Founders truly believed that if they did not specifically design their new government to operate independently of religion, then religion would come to influence policy. Safeguards were necessary, and they were implemented.

In order to understand the ideology that produced the United States Constitution, you have to go back to an English agitator, a Brit named John Locke.

LOCKE-ED AND LOADED

If John Locke had gone on tour, Thomas Jefferson would've camped out overnight for tickets. The philosopher—also a medical researcher and Oxford academic—had been born into a Puritan family in Somerset, England, during a tumultuous time in the country's history: a religious war was roiling between the Protestants, Catholics, and Anglicans, and British politics were confused, to say the least. Monarchy as a ruling institution had come and it had gone, then it had come back again. Conflicts between Parliament and the monarchy were ongoing, and religious conflicts continued unabated.

It was out of this period of religious passions, political ambitions, and attempts to meld the two that Locke's revolutionary ideas began to take shape. He began to promote the individual's search for truth rather than the old standby: let the institutions tell you what you think. Use reason, he warned, not faith. Discern between legitimate functions of government and religious institutions and illegitimate functions.

In 1690, he penned "Essay Concerning Human Understanding," a now classic work of philosophy in which he outlined his theory of human knowledge. However, it was his political writings that moved men like Thomas Jefferson, and which set the stage for the American Revolution. The first treatise in Locke's *Two Treatises of Government* was a refutation of the monarchy's claim of authority over its subjects, at least in the terms laid out by Sir Robert Filmer, who argued that the monarch's authority was that of a father over his children.

More influential to the inchoate American revolutionaries was Locke's second treatise, in which he laid out his view of societies: they emerge, Locke wrote, when individuals make a figurative "contract" to submit themselves to a ruler. Locke was in opposition to our friend Hobbes when he argued that the ruler's right to rule is given to him by the ruled on trust, and that if that trust is broken, the ruler can and should be deposed. He believed that humans could follow rational principles.

Locke's ideal government stayed out of the people's way, doing only what was absolutely critical for the common good and leaving the rest to individuals. It stopped citizens from harming one another and protected private property, but otherwise stayed out of its people's hair.

Locke's influence hung like cigar smoke over the Constitutional Convention. He was an intellectual rock star to the Framers, who agreed with his call for limited and restrained government. Harvard political scientist Louis Hartz, writing in 1955, said, "Locke dominates American political thought as no thinker anywhere dominates the political thought of a nation."

Echoes of Locke resound throughout the words and writing of the Founding Fathers; John Adams drew upon the second treatise in 1780 when he was writing the preamble to the Massachusetts Constitution. James Madison consulted the work of the Philosopher of Freedom while shaping the Constitution. Jefferson put Locke among his list of top three greatest human beings, and shamelessly cribbed Locke's ideas for the Declaration of Independence. In fact,

Jefferson practically plagiarized Locke when he assembled the text of the document.

From the second essay of John Locke's 1690 treatise "Concerning Civil Government":

> *Such revolutions happen not upon every little mismanagement in public affairs. Great mistakes in the ruling part, many wrong and inconvenient laws, and all the slips of human frailty will be borne by the people without mutiny or murmur. But if a long train of abuses, prevarications, and artifices, all tending the same way, make the design visible to the people, and they cannot but feel what they lie under, and see whither they are going, it is not to be wondered that they should then rouse themselves, and endeavor to put the rule into such hands which may secure to them the end for which government was at first erected.*

From the Declaration of Independence:

> *Prudence, indeed, will dictate that Governments long established should not be changed for light and transient causes; and accordingly all experience hath shown, that mankind are more disposed to suffer, while evils are sufferable, than to right themselves by abolishing the forms to which they are accustomed. But when a long train of abuses and usurpations, pursuing invariably the same Object evinces a design to reduce them under absolute Despotism, it is their right, it is their duty, to throw off such Government, and to provide new Guards for their future security.*

Locke's writings directly refute the idea of a religious government. A religious government would oversee and meddle in much that is personal, such as marriage and individual worship. In addition, it would oversee these personal activities using a narrow definition provided by a particular faith—or a broad collection of faiths. Locke's writings were, in fact, a direct attack on the idea of the "Christian Commonwealth" framed around the idea that government should be intertwined with Christian belief and symbolism. According to Locke:

> *Laws provide simply that the goods and health of subjects be not injured by the fraud and the violence of others. . . . The business of law is not to provide for the truth of opinion, but for the safety and security of the commonwealth and of every particular man's goods and persons. The truth is not taught by law, nor has she any need of force to procure her entrance into the minds of men.*

It was Locke's ideas that spurred Thomas Jefferson and James Madison to create the 1786 Virginia "Statute for Religious Freedom," which specified that no religious test could be applied to those seeking public office. This local statute inspired the Constitution's clause about religious tests—one of the key controversies that swirled around the document during the fight for its ratification.

THE "GODLESS" CONSTITUTION

The ratification of the U.S. Constitution was itself a deliberate break from the state/religion partnership that defined so many

European governments in the preceding centuries. Prior to the Enlightenment, it was generally understood that church and state supported one another, propped up one another, and joined forces to keep the masses out of power and to keep them subdued and cowed by fear (fear of God on the one hand, fear of the police and military on the other). Church leaders wielded devastating political power, and regularly used faith as a weapon to condemn "heretics" who challenged their secular interests.

And so, when the fifty-five exhausted men emerged from Philadelphia's Independence Hall on September 17, 1787, to announce the creation and signing of a new Constitution to replace the flimsy Articles of Confederation, religious power players of the era were scandalized.

The new document, far from acknowledging Christianity as the supreme religion of the land, and invoking God's protection and supremacy, didn't mention the Creator at all. This hardly seemed possible, at the time. It was, at the time, nearly unthinkable.

Someone asked Alexander Hamilton about the oversight. One story suggests that he replied that the new nation was not in need of "foreign aid"; according to another, he simply said: "We forgot."[33]

Using Lockean ideas, the Constitution effectively built a wall between organized religion and secular government. This was no blooper, either: in the Declaration of Independence, God only gets two quick mentions—a reference to "the Laws of Nature and Nature's God," and the line about how men are "endowed by their Creator with certain inalienable rights."

He crops up only twice in the eighty-five Federalist Papers, and the only substantial reference to religion in the Papers is less than flattering. Madison, writing in No. 10, argues that aggressive pursuit of religious opinions causes men to "vex and oppress each other."[34]

With all this in the historical record, it's interesting to read contemporary literature distributed by James Dobson's ultra-right-wing Focus on the Family that has tried to capitalize on general ignorance of Constitutional history by claiming "the Constitution was designed to perpetuate a Christian order."

This is a favorite religious right talking point: the Founding Fathers were religious as hell; America is a fundamentally Christian country; we've fallen from grace by ignoring their godly designs.

This is, of course, bullshit. At the time the Constitution was ratified, the document was mercilessly attacked by the powerful religious figures of the age, who considered its lack of Christian backbone a threat to their own influence. The Pennsylvania pamphleteer and Constitution critic "Aristocrotis" (a pen name) wrote the following criticism in 1788:

"[The] new Constitution, disdains . . . belief of a deity, the immortality of the soul, or the resurrection of the body, a day of judgment, or a future state of rewards and punishment."

Not exactly a churchly blessing for a document allegedly "designed to perpetuate a Christian order."

What happened in Philadelphia to set the country on such a clear path toward secular government, where religion is allowed to flourish but not be mixed up with government? In stark contrast to later political movements, the Founders had no interest in snuffing religion out; they had a great deal of regard for it. It was this very respect for religion, in fact, that led them to carve out a safe shelter for it, away from the hands of the power-hungry and cynical.

What is frequently overlooked—deliberately, by right-wing

historians—is that the Founding Fathers were direct products of and active participants in the Enlightenment, the movement of rationalism, pragmatism, science, and individual rights that swept through eighteenth-century Europe. While some factions of the Enlightenment were antireligion* or even atheist in nature, the Founders themselves tended to emphasize the importance of free thought and personal conscience over any single dogma.

"Let the human mind loose," John Adams wrote. "It must be loose. It will be loose. Superstition and dogmatism cannot confine it."[35] Adams condemned the old medieval idea of a state where the "priesthood had enveloped the feudal monarch in clouds and mysteries."

In their struggle to fit the newly independent United States to a legal framework, the Framers were less concerned with strangling the proponents of a theocracy than keeping them safely tucked out of the way. The Framers—no strangers to inspired and novel leaps of thought—argued that the best way to protect religion was to spirit it away from the tentacles of political power that tend to corrupt whatever they touch, that if religion and state are kept separate, there will be far more legitimate religious freedom, as there is much less state interest in squashing worship when that worship has nothing to do with exercising power.

On the other hand, the Framers also anticipated the danger of allowing national leaders to push for policies that were "blessed in the name of God." The problem is less with following the Word of God than with determining what exactly that Word might be, after

---

*The Enlightenment ideal of reason and logic triumphing over emotion and blind faith was perhaps most saucily summarized by French Enlightenment philosopher Denis Diderot, who wrote: "Men will never be free until the last king is strangled with the entrails of the last priest."

all the translations, opportunistic hijacking, bigoted interpretation, and learned discussions. James Madison, writing in the Federalist Papers, expressed this most clearly when he suggested that God's word is rendered "dim and doubtful" in the Bible.

And so, the Constitution is, by design, a God-less document. When the Constitution was drafted, members of the era's "religious right" were appalled that the Constitution prohibited religious tests for holding public office. They were shocked that Quakers were allowed to "affirm" rather than "swear" their oaths of office.

One article that was published in response to the new Constitution appeared in the *New York Daily Advertiser*. It neatly summed up the objections many raised against the no-religious-test Article 6. The article, which favored religious tests (if you couldn't tell) described the sorts of people that these tests were designed to keep out of power:

> *1st. Quakers, who will make the blacks saucy, and at the same time deprive us of the means of defence—2dly. Mahometans [Muslims], who ridicule the doctrine of the Trinity—3dly. Deists, abominable wretches—4thly. Negroes, the seed of Cain—5thly. Beggars, who when set on horseback will ride to the devil—6thly. Jews etc. etc.*

The article was popular enough to be reprinted and republished within days throughout the Northeast. But George Washington defended the Godless Constitution, telling a cheesed-off group of Presbyterian ministers and elders that he thought "the path of true piety is so plain as to require but little political direction."

Despite the venomous attacks in the press, religious reaction to the Constitution was not universally condemnatory. Many religious sects, which felt politically vulnerable and simply wanted to worship in peace, supported the document.

The supreme irony of the age—at least in retrospect—is that the Baptists of New England (a much persecuted sect at the time) fought harder than anyone against the overlap of religion and government. They feared the influence of rival and bigoted sects. And thus, separating government and church wasn't considered by the Baptists, and other religious groups like them, as an antireligious move.

THOMAS JEFFERSON, DOGMA HUNTER

Thomas Jefferson didn't attend the Constitutional Convention (he was in France at the time) but his influence was felt in Philadelphia. Although he was largely satisfied with the agreement that emerged from the Convention, he was disturbed by the lack of any specific guarantee of religious freedom, spurring his ongoing fight for a Bill of Rights to protect individual liberties in the absence of any constitutional language to serve that purpose.

Jefferson's fearless opposition to religious dogma and his championing the separation of church and state would return to haunt him in the spring of 1800, when he battled John Adams for the presidency. His old rival Alexander Hamilton (himself quite irreligious) joined politicized clergymen in their attacks on Jefferson.

The Gazette of the United States put the thrust of the assault quite plainly:

THE GRAND QUESTION STATED. At the present solemn moment the only question to be asked by every American, laying his hand on his heart, is "Shall I continue in allegiance to GOD—AND A RELIGIOUS PRESIDENT; or impiously declare for JEFFERSON—AND NO GOD!!!"[36]

Thomas Jefferson hated this kind of crap. One of his best known lines, words that resonate with an awe-inspiring power, appear on the rotunda of the Jefferson Memorial in Washington, D.C.:

"I have sworn upon the altar of God eternal hostility against every form of tyranny over the mind of man."

Pop quiz. These words were written in reference to:

a. King George III of England, against whom the Founding Fathers struggled during the Revolutionary War.

b. Louis XVI of France, the target of the briefly glorious but kinda bloody French Revolution.

c. A group of clergymen in Philadelphia who were denouncing Jefferson from the pulpit during his race for the presidency against John Adams.

If you answered c, you get a slice of pecan pie. The "tyranny" here is the tyranny of clergymen using their connection with God to bully their followers into voting for a particular candidate. The condemnation of faith-based politics is etched forever onto Jefferson's monument, as it should be.

The Bush White House website begins its Jefferson biography with this same "altar of God" quote. Not surprisingly, of course, it omits any reference to the actual context of the quote.

> *In the thick of party conflict in 1800, Thomas Jefferson*
> *wrote in a private letter, "I have sworn upon the altar of*
> *God eternal hostility against every form of tyranny over the*
> *mind of man."*
> *This powerful advocate of liberty was born in 1743 in*
> *Albermarle County, Virginia.*

After reading the above selection, you might reasonably conclude that Jefferson, a deeply religious man, was jotting down some randomly inspirational thoughts to a pen pal. The website features not even a passing reference to Jefferson's feeling about state and religion in the entire biography—which was, of course, written and posted with your tax dollars.

But evasive biographies of our Founders are not the only thing your tax dollars are paying for.

"FAITH-BASED" OR POLITICS-BASED?

One of the most visible manifestations of the increasingly porous wall between church and state is the sudden surge in funding for "faith-based" organizations. Funding "faith-based" groups has been a goal of Conservative Christians and a strategy used by Republicans that has paid serious dividends in terms of the votes and dollars that have poured in from the increasingly well-organized far right.

This has been an extremely sound electoral strategy, both for canny and calculating Republican political operatives such as the not-so-religious Karl Rove, and for canny and calculating religious political operatives such as Pat Robertson and James Dobson.

Garry Wills, writing in the October 6, 2005, issue of *The New*

York Review of Books, detailed what he described as the religious "fringe government" currently in ascendance. Among the most unnerving trends that he details is the ever-strengthening bridge between hard-line Catholics and politicized evangelicals, and the cynical (if mutually beneficial) ways in which the White House uses these groups as a political weapon.

This trend isn't merely a coming together of like-minded people of faith, striving to find common ground. Instead, it is a sign of the extent to which a headline version of religion is now directly and unapologetically calling the shots within the halls of a nominally secular government of a multifaith (and nonfaith) society on issues such as "Intelligent Design" and stem-cell research. It is a disturbing development because reactionary Catholic leaders including Father Richard John Neuhaus and Archbishop Raymond Burke of St. Louis have, in the midst of a heated election campaign, advocated such outrageously political conflations of faith and power as denying John Kerry communion for having supported legalized abortion . . .

Some of the most vivid manifestations of faith-based politics cropped up—when else—during the aftermath of the Hurricane Katrina disaster. Instead of putting federal dollars to work rebuilding homes or rebuilding levees after the disaster, FEMA pumped money into reimbursing faith-based organizations, including churches, for the resources expended helping flood victims. The payments—made with taxpayer money—mark the first time that the government has made such payments to faith-based groups at a time following natural disasters, *The Washington Post* reported in September 2005. Further, if you happened to be an atheist, your tax dollars may have been reimbursing the Catholic Church. If you were a Unitarian, a chunk of your hard-earned paycheck might have gone into the coffers of a church that refuses to recognize gay unions.

Friend of the outraged, Thomas Paine memorably took the ostensibly peaceful Quakers of the colonies to task in an appendix of *Common Sense*. The appendix was published in later editions as a response to the writings of Quaker leaders that were issued in reaction to *Common Sense*. The polemics argued against Paine's revolutionary rhetoric (in a pamphlet succinctly titled "The Ancient Testimony and Principles of the people called Quakers renewed, with Respect to the King and Government, and touching the Commotions now prevailing in these and other parts of America, addressed to the People in General").

After taking apart with surgical precision the Quaker argument against war with England, Paine then went on to make any Quaker opposed to independence look like an obsequious, kowtowing Anglophile hot for tyranny and eager for emasculation.

But after wishing the Quakers "every civil and religious right," he ends his tract with this prophetic wish: "But that the example which ye have unwisely set, of mingling religion with politics, *may be disavowed and reprobated by every inhabitant of AMERICA.*"

In the Bush administration, however, the only disavowing and reprobation going on is of administration critics and international watchdog groups. The mingling has reached a fever pitch.

The intrusion of personal faith into public policy is even more alarming when it begins to affect questions of foreign policy. Bob Woodward captured a startling new paradigm for American leadership in his 2003 book *Bush at War*.

"[The President is] casting his mission and that of the country in the grand vision of God's master plan."[37]

For anyone who knows American history, that is a scary suggestion. Five days after the September 11 attacks, Bush said, "This *crusade*, this war on terrorism, is going to take a while" (italics mine).

The message seemed to catch on with the troops, too. The Deputy Undersecretary of Defense for Intelligence, Lieutenant General William "Jerry" Boykin, caught crusade fever in a big way.

The Delta Force vet is an outspoken evangelical Christian. He appeared in uniform before a religious group in Oregon in June 2004 to declare that radical Islamists hate America "because we're a Christian nation, because our foundation and our roots are Judeo-Christian . . . and the enemy is a guy named Satan."[38]

Talking about a fight against a Muslim warlord in Somalia, Boykin told another audience, "I knew my God was bigger than his. I knew that my God was a real God and his was an idol."[39]

Boykin's comments have reverberated worldwide, immediately making their way into the anti-American dialogue that continues to feed Al Qaeda's coffers and recruitment offices. It was about as disastrous a remark as an American government employee could possibly make. Boykin's comments about President Bush also make the greatest hits reel from 2003: "Why is this man in the White House? The majority of Americans did not vote for him. Why is he there? And I tell you this morning that he's in the White House because God put him there for a time such as this."[40] Of course, such thinking flies directly in the face of the Enlightenment values this country was founded upon. The president is very much not a divinely protected monarch, fulfilling a mystical mission of godly justice. He is, by the standards set by the men who designed the Office of President, a Lockean leader whose office is given to him by the people on the basis of trust. That is, God didn't put George Bush in the White House. The citizens of the United States did. And when that trust is broken, the Founders believed if they followed Locke, the office might rightly be taken away from him.

Dogma Versus Science

In a triumph of Orwellian wordsmithing, so-called creationists have successfully pushed a nonscientific, fairy-tale version of evolution onto the curriculum of several American school boards, using the term "Intelligent Design."

Intelligent Design (or ID, as it's known among its fans) claims that life is just so darn complicated that physical adaptations among mammals and other life forms are just so mind-boggling and im-probable that some Great Interior Designer must have assembled it.

"There are natural systems that cannot be adequately explained in terms of undirected natural forces," leading ID proponent William Dembski said, "and that exhibit features which in any other cir-cumstance we would attribute to intelligence."[41] Intelligent Design is a collection of vague speculation that "fills in" gaps in existing sci-entific theories. Evolutionary theory? Nothing more than a guess.

In fact, the theory of evolution, as anyone who completed tenth-grade biology before the new curriculum standards in Kansas took effect knows, is no mere guess. It started out as a hypothesis. When it was proven by experiments that could be replicated, it grew into a theory. Because the hypothesis of ID cannot be disproven by ex-periments, it is not "falsifiable"—that is, not designed to be tested by evidence. You either believe it or you don't. What that means, then, is that ID is a "faith-based" idea.

This sort of debate has its place in a church, a private home, or an AA meeting. It could even be a marginally justifiable inclusion in any world history class, also a required course for high schoolers across the country. But it is so far from the accepted definition of science that in order to allow ID to be taught in its classrooms, the state of Kansas had to adopt weaker science standards for its science curriculum.

Luckily for Bobby Henderson, those weaker science standards lowered the bar so far that his "Flying Spaghetti Monster" theory of creation fit right in. In 2005, the twentysomething Corvallis, Oregon, resident decided to invent a theory of creation in order to put ID-adopting school boards to the test. The challenge: How is your idea about an "Intelligent Designer" any more scientifically valid than my idea about a flying spaghetti monster creating the universe? And if it isn't any more scientific, how do you defend inserting your idea into the curriculum without inserting mine? So far, the validity of Henderson's monster has not been tested. Nor has the theory of Intelligent Design.*

Fans of science can rejoice, at least a little bit, at the example locals in Dover, Pennsylvania, set in November 2005. Pissed-off voters ousted a pro–Intelligent Design school board and replaced them with a school board whose members believed in teaching science in science class. The next month, to add insult to injury, a federal district court ruled that ID couldn't be mentioned in science classes in the Dover school district.

Judge John Jones concluded in his decision that ID is not science.

---

*On a similar front: *The Onion* elegantly nailed the crux of the discussion with a 2005 article that described a government initiative to introduce the "Intelligent Falling" theory into classrooms to give students an alternative to the scientifically falsifiable "Theory of Gravity."

"We find that the secular purposes claimed by the Board amount to a pretext for the Board's real purpose, which was to promote religion in the public school classroom," the conservative, Christian judge wrote in his scathing 139-page opinion.

"It is ironic that several of these individuals, who so staunchly and proudly touted their religious convictions in public, would time and again lie to cover their tracks and disguise the real purpose behind the ID Policy," he wrote.*

Now if only Kansas would get with the program.

A person concerned with issues of the separation of church and state might find such parochial battles amusing but not necessarily threatening. Let the states fight it out among themselves, he might argue, if he were of an antifederalist bent. But in August 2005, George W. Bush weighed in on the controversy, and that's when things started getting dangerous.

"You're asking me whether or not people ought to be exposed to different ideas," the president told a roundtable group of Texas reporters. "The answer is yes." While not overtly promoting ID over the theory of evolution, Bush was making it clear that he was in favor of creating a place for the hypothesis in America's classrooms, alongside the teaching of evolution. (But taking the president's words at face value means good news for Bobby Henderson, too.)

The push by Christian conservatives to get religion into public, taxpayer-funded schools—and their success in persuading their president to openly endorse the teaching of religious doctrine in science classrooms across the country—lead one straight to James Madison.

---

*The full text of Judge Jones's opinion can be read at www.aclupa.org/downloads/Dec20 opinion.pdf.

SILENT ACCUMULATIONS
AND ENCROACHMENTS

The Founders were agronomists, such as George Washington; linguists and archaeologists, such as Thomas Jefferson; inventors and physicists, such as Ben Franklin. They understood that the public realm—which includes education and government—must be populated with facts. Religion, they believed, was part of the community and part of the individual's private life, and while they respected its place in society, they were eminently aware of the damage it could do to rational and scientific thought in certain circumstances.

But it was James Madison, more than the others, who identified the danger of sectarianism, especially religious sectarianism. Interestingly, Madison's views on religion have been invoked by both the left and the right wing in debates about church and state. And there's good reason for this. He played both sides of the fence.

As a young man, Madison was fairly outspoken about his own Christian beliefs. Privately, he worried about "Heaven" and "testimony" and "being fervent advocates in the cause of Christ." Unlike Jefferson, he proclaimed national days of prayer during his term as president.

But as he grew older, accumulated more political experience, and had more time to think on the matter, Madison began a slow retreat from these positions. While as a younger man he had favored instituting chaplains in Congress, as an older gentleman Madison suggested that doing this sort of thing—or issuing proclamations for national days of anything religious—was likely unconstitutional.

In "Detached Memoranda," one of his assorted writings, col-lected along with the miscellany of other Founders in *The Founders' Constitution*, Madison anticipated some of the religion-in-politics problems we face today:

> *The danger of silent accumulations & encroachments by Ecclesiastical Bodies have not sufficiently engaged attention in the U.S. They have the noble merit of first unshackling the conscience from persecuting laws, and of establishing among religious Sects a legal equality.*

Madison was even more prescient when he spoke to the peril of religious organizations amassing wealth and property:

> *But besides the danger of a direct mixture of Religion & civil Government, there is an evil which ought to be guarded agst in the indefinite accumulation of property from the capacity of holding it in perpetuity by ecclesiasti-cal corporations. The power of all corporations, ought to be limited in this respect. The growing wealth acquired by them never fails to be a source of abuses.*

In a letter to Edward Livingston in 1822, Madison wrote that "an alliance or coalition between Government and religion cannot be too carefully guarded against. Every new and successful example therefore of a perfect separation between ecclesiastical and civil matters is of importance . . . religion and government will exist in greater purity, without (rather) than with the aid of government."[42]

Was Madison a flip-flopper? Or had he taken time to allow his position to mature and marinate? When John Kerry expressed similarly evolving views about the war in Iraq—with the benefit of new information and shifting events in the Middle East— he was labeled as a guy who couldn't "stay the course." The Republican character assassins who turned a decorated veteran into a weak-willed coward were right in one abstract sense: it is possible to hold too many opinions and be fatally indecisive. It's a pity that the countercharge never stuck: that rigid thinking and an unwillingness to accept new evidence can be as deadly as spinning in circles.

THE ASSAULT ON SCIENCE

While Intelligent Design merely threatens the future of science education, and the minds of our nation's children, other dogma-based administration decisions to suppress science are proving far more serious.

Consider the following case studies. Unsurprisingly, there is a common theme that runs through all of them: good science proves that a particular approach or treatment will improve or even save lives. Right-wing Christians then deem these approaches or treatments "immoral." The administration then suppresses public science in support of its followers' religious beliefs. Interestingly, and perhaps not coincidentally, all of these case studies have to do with the health of women—both in America and around the world.

SCIENCE SAYS: The best way to fight AIDS in Africa is by a combination of condom distribution and education about the various risk factors that lead to contracting HIV/AIDS.

GOD "SAYS": It is always wrong to have extramarital sex. Condoms encourage extramarital sex. Let AIDS kill those who sin against me! And for all those Republican congressmen who cheated on their wives during their last term—a free pass. For now. Just don't anger me by keeping abortion safe and legal.

HOW IT PLAYED OUT: With the Pitts Amendment to the Bush Emergency Plan for AIDS Relief (PEPFAR), the GOP-controlled Congress earmarked 33 percent of AIDS-prevention funds for unproven "abstinence until marriage" programs. The Smith Amendment allowed federally funded "faith-based" groups to refuse to provide information about proven methods of protection against HIV/AIDS or even to make referrals to clinics or organizations that offer critical prevention services. U.S.-funded groups are now also allowed to denigrate the benefits of condom use.

SCIENCE SAYS: The "Plan B" or "morning-after" pill is a safe way for women—including victims of rape and incest—to use contraception. The FDA's own scientists, in fact, have declared the pill a contraceptive, not an abortifacient.

GOD "SAYS": Contraception offends me, regardless of the state of the mother's health or the circumstances under which she became pregnant! Let the women become pregnant and multiply!

HOW IT PLAYED OUT: In May 2004, anonymous top federal drug officials rejected an application to allow over-the-counter sales of the morning-after pill . . . months before a government scientific review of the application was completed.

The New York Times reported that congressional investigators "had been unable to uncover the role in the Plan B decision played by the former agency commissioner, Dr. Mark B. McClellan,* because agency officials told investigators that all of his e-mail messages and written correspondence on the subject had been deleted or thrown out. The Democrats charged that these acts contravened federal records laws."[43]

SCIENCE SAYS: A new cervical cancer vaccine has been proven to be nearly 100 percent effective—it should be part of the standard roster of shots received by young women. The cancer is spurred, in part, by the sexually transmitted papilloma virus.

GOD "SAYS": Cancer, schmancer! There is an issue of grave importance at stake—and I know I'm going to seem kind of obsessed with it, but: premarital and extramarital sex! Come on, folks, cervical cancer is yet another weapon in my arsenal. You sleep around, I give you cancer. Easy.

HOW IT PLAYED OUT: Still pending, but the relevant officials are consulting people such as Gene Rudd, the associate executive director of the Christian Medical & Dental Associations. "Parents should have the choice," Rudd told *The Washington Post*. "There are those who would say, 'We can provide a better, healthier alternative than the vaccine, and that is to teach abstinence.' "[44]

---

*White House press secretary Scott McClellan's brother.

REBUILDING THE WALL

There is no need to choose between good science and passionate religion. Many of the world's best scientists—Newton and Einstein are famous examples—swear by their personal beliefs in a higher power.

But there is a need to decide whether the nation wants a theocratic government, taking direction from the mullahs of the Christian right, or a secular government that respects and protects religion while letting rational debate determine national policy.

In 1803, Madison struck at the heart of this debate when he said, "The purpose of separation of church and state is to keep forever from these shores the ceaseless strife that has soaked the soil of Europe in blood for centuries."

Madison grasped the most elemental danger of combining church and state: when you bring religion into the debate, suddenly you're not arguing about the most pragmatic course of action for a community to take; you're arguing about whose faith is right. By turning the Republican Party into the Christian/Ariel Sharon* Party, the administration has turned away from the roots of American tradition—with potentially terrible long-term consequences, such as increasingly religious-based parties fighting about belief instead of policy, a resurgence of religious intolerance, and an utter destruction of the secular nation-state ideal that has served America quite well for a couple centuries now.

---

*At the time this book went to press, Ariel Sharon was incapacitated by a stroke. References to Sharon here specifically address Sharonist policies vis-à-vis partition of the West Bank and a policy of military aggression toward, rather than economic and diplomatic engagement with, the Palestinian people as a whole.

So let's do a quick rundown:

THE FOUNDERS

- Revered science, and made the establishment of universities one of their many priorities for the country.
- Deliberately protected religion with the Bill of Rights while repudiating the "Christian Commonwealth" concept with the Constitution.
- Battled religious activists who wanted to desecularize government.

BUSH AND FRIENDS

- Have regularly gutted science anytime it runs contrary to the dogma of the religious right.
- Have assaulted religion's protected role in the United States by exposing it to criticism by Americans who don't like seeing their own rights abridged in the name of someone else's faith.
- Battled secular activists who want to keep the wall between church and state intact.

This sort of thing puts the modern conservative movement in a real bind. Arguing in support of Supreme Court nominee Samuel Alito, Karl Rove said in November 2005: "Our arguments will carry the day because the force and logic and wisdom of the Founders, all of them, are on our side."[45]

Actually, the contrast between the cynical political manipulators of religion—such as Rove—and the Founders couldn't be starker than on the issue of church and state. Who loses when the far-right Christian activist vision becomes the model for American government?

Religious minorities lose. If you're not a fundamentalist Christian, a dogmatic conservative Catholic, or a pro-Sharon Jew, your views and beliefs will not be respected. You're one of the unpopular, unimportant religions.

Science loses. Whenever science and Christian fundamentalism come to blows, the administration has always gone where the votes and dollars are, regardless of how many people (usually women) may be hurt or killed as a result.

Education loses. The concept: It's fine to educate children with the facts as long as those facts don't contradict the religious dogma of one particularly vocal group of voters. It's pretty easy to make the argument that America needs more world-respected scientists, not fewer.

And far-right Christian activists lose, too. Because when their views are forced upon a nation that doesn't agree with them, in the form of laws made by a supposedly secular government, they will be blamed for the disastrous aftereffects. As delicious as that sounds, it's not a good reason to stand idly by.

THE Alternate Universe DAILY SPECTATOR

SEPTEMBER 8, 2002

Caution Urged on WMD Claims

WASHINGTON, D.C.—Does Saddam have them, or not? The "them" in question are weapons of mass destruction. And the question is open because no corroborated reports of their existence have yet surfaced in the media or publicly accessible government reports.

Neoconservative commentators and political appointees, in their bid to push for an invasion of Iraq and the toppling of Saddam Hussein, have leaked several seemingly damning reports by Hussein regime defectors. The reports seem to indicate evidence of both biological and chemical weapons in Iraq, and troubling evidence pointing toward an active nuclear program.

But an internal administration investigation has divulged that much of the WMD information streaming into the media is coming from Ahmed Chalabi and his organization, the Iraqi National Congress. President Bush, addressing the country from Washington, took the unusual step of addressing the intelligence controversy directly and seeking to cool the debate.

"A lot of good Americans are worried, saying Iraq's got WMD, and maybe something's got to be done. But we don't know that there are WMD in there. Inspectors haven't found them. And, more and more, it's looking as though a group headed by Ahmed Chalabi, a convicted embezzler and known con man, is the source of many of these new allegations. We need to be careful about taking this man's word for it, because the implications are grave."

Bush added that a second full-on war was the last thing that America needed.

"We're already fighting one in Afghanistan, against the Taliban deadenders. I don't think anyone wants to see American troops dying in Baghdad or Najaf because of bad intelligence. Remember what Ben Franklin said about war: 'There never was a good war or a bad peace.'"

Bush, who didn't serve in combat during Vietnam, is said to be sensitive about putting American lives at risk for anything less than clearly justified reasons. "He's terrified of making a mistake and ordering men to their deaths because of bad information or an emotional decision," said a White House insider who asked to remain anonymous. "The historical irony would be devastating."

SIX

THE RISE OF THE SUPERMEN

We're an empire now, and when we act, we create our own reality. And while you're studying that reality—judiciously, as you will—we'll act again, creating other new realities, which you can study too, and that's how things will sort out. We're history's actors . . . and you, all of you, will be left to just study what we do.

—Senior White House aide, as quoted by Ron Suskind
in *The New York Times Magazine,* October 17, 2004

To err, is the lot of humanity, and never for a moment, have I ever had the presumption to suppose that I had not a full proportion of it.

—George Washington, draft of Farewell Address,
May 15, 1796

THE FOUNDING FATHERS nursed profound doubt, collectively, about whether any kind of earthly paradise could be created using zealous works and fearsome laws. Human beings, they reasoned, were fallible and government and church both potentially dangerous institutions. The only reliable answer was to seek more information and err on the side of being humane.

Now that godly faith is (at least in name) in cultural and political ascendancy, you would expect some of the following approaches to be wise approaches:

A HUMBLER GOVERNMENT: Since we are all small before God's great works, it would follow that the fallibility of man (and his leaders) is explicit, and accountability is expected of all. The slightest trace of serious wrongdoing should be enough to produce a guilt-inspired resignation—investigations shouldn't even be necessary once the stink of impropriety has settled upon a public servant's office.

HESITATION TO TAKE HUMAN LIFE RECKLESSLY: as that is God's domain. A government-sponsored movement against war, the death penalty, AIDS prevention programs that are more about dogma than saving lives. Life is more sacred than taboos, right?

AN OVERWHELMING CONCERN FOR THE POOREST AMERICANS: indeed, for struggling people all over the world—whom Jesus went to a lot of trouble to talk about and stick up for all over the New Testament.

The value of conventional morality seems to be self-evident—if people are moral, conflict and inequality recedes, and society as a whole prospers. But throughout history, people have been willing to proclaim themselves—or entire classes of human beings—beyond the confines of mundane morality. The concept of the philosopher-king, who uses superior insight and wisdom to rule unchallenged over a society of virtual slaves, dates back to Plato's Republic—and earlier, to priestly castes who dominated ancient societies in the Middle East and Africa. Come to think of it, it was secret knowledge, interpreted and manipulated by an elite, that was the sort of thing the Christian Church used to keep everybody down before the Protestant Reformation.

This sort of thing turned the stomachs of Enlightenment thinkers such as the Founding Fathers. Their end goal was equality—the goal was protection of all free-thinking individuals, not the empowerment of a tiny exclusive clique.

"It is essential to [a republic] that it be derived from the great body of the society, not from an inconsiderable proportion or favored class of it," James Madison wrote in *Federalist No. 39*.

By contrast, you can—and many political conspiracy theorists will—trace a direct line from Plato through philosopher Friedrich Nietzsche (who wrote of the intellectually unstoppable, post-morality "superman" or "New Man") through University of Chicago professor and "neoconservative" guru Leo Strauss through his politically active disciples who still exercise a great deal of pull in American foreign policy circles.

And you can—and many political conspiracy theorists will—point out that it's very unusual that a group of Strauss-educated and/or influenced officials were absolutely pivotal in leading the charge for war in Iraq, a charge launched well before September 11 and the WMD craze conjured in order to gain the political means to get the job done.

In short: It's possible that Strauss-influenced neocons following a doctrine of "necessary lies" were instrumental in crafting the war in Iraq to propagate an American world-empire controlled by a cabal of cackling fascists with an unhealthy obsession with the darker bits of *Thus Spake Zarathustra*.

Or it's possible that the neocons, who saw U.S.- and Likud-powered Israeli security as closely linked, viewed taking out

Saddam as the first domino in a wave of democratization that would better the Middle East and U.S. security prospects, and just naturally helped one another out as they steered the otherwise rudderless ship of U.S. foreign policy after 9/11.

Here's the thing: It doesn't really matter. Because either way, the war on Iraq was an aggressive—not a defensive—war sold by a tightly run campaign of deliberate misinformation (cramming "Al Qaeda," "WMD," and "Saddam" into as many public statements as possible, carefully crafting the linking words so as to avoid technical lies), fear-mongering, and the occasional whopper. Intelligence was cooked and garnished to the order of neocon chefs. The gears of war churned not because of a concern about terrorism, but because of a golden opportunity to accomplish a long-standing foreign policy goal.

America's Declaration of Independence states that every nation is entitled to a "separate and equal station" among "the powers of the earth." The Enlightenment political philosophers—and the Founding Fathers—argued that no nation has any right to conquer or interfere in the affairs of any other nation, except for self-defense.

In the draft of his farewell address, George Washington wrote, after stressing the dangers of entangling alliances:

> *[I ardently wish] that we may be always prepared for War, but never unsheath the sword except in self-defence so long as Justice and our essential rights, and national respectability can be preserved without it.*

The Founders even had doubts about the wisdom of something we take for granted today—a strong national peacetime army. James Madison, in *Federalist No. 41,* wrote:

America united, with a handful of troops, or without a single soldier, exhibits a more forbidding posture to foreign ambition than America disunited, with a hundred thousand veterans ready for combat.

Leaders such as Washington didn't have to delude their men into fighting on false pretenses, because their cause was self-evidently just. The American Revolution was the culmination of decades of grievances, economic pressure, and passionate arguments. It was the fruit of years of debate by relatively free men who yearned to be far freer. There were volumes of intellectual discourse about the fundamental nature of a free society, and the blueprint for revolution was in the hands of everyone.

By contrast, the reasons for invading Iraq were debated (if at all) by a small group of power-players acting behind the scenes. The real argument about Iraq wasn't whether it was a mortal threat—it was whether the U.S. should depose a dictator in order to effect utopian change in one of the most volatile and dangerous regions on earth. In the "name of Democracy." In the name of the ideals of George Washington, Thomas Jefferson, Alexander Hamilton, Benjamin Franklin, John Adams, and Thomas Paine.

And American citizens were never given the opportunity to hear an open, candid debate about the reasons the government would be asking their sons and daughters to risk their lives—in more than two thousand cases, *give* their lives—for their country.

The Bush administration's actions in the prelude to the Iraq war weren't those of a depraved individual, a wronged son out for revenge. But instead, they were the actions of a group of men and women who consider themselves smart enough to see "the big picture." And the Big Picture promises so much that is positive, in the eyes of the neocons, that thoroughly immoral acts are justified. The ends justify the means. It's a trap, which inspires even the most brilliant people to do truly contemptible things.

There is a kind of humility inherent in the act of laying yourself at the feet of certain maxims—treating prisoners decently, telling the truth, owning up to mistakes, holding even dear friends accountable for failing the public. You are saying: "Even though I think my goals are more important than observing this abstract ritual (not lying, not abusing the innocent, not dodging accountability), I hereby sublimate them to the greater principle of humility before a serious moral code."

The reverse—depraved moral relativism—can lead to sticky situations.

- "We used despicable means to destroy the election hopes of John McCain, a decent man and a war hero. Still, we had to do it, because his brand of conservatism is corrupt and would hurt America in the long run. Our brand of conservatism will make sure that the country is more stable, and that business is protected." OR
- "We used despicable means to goad the country into war with Iraq. Still, we had to do it, because once Iraq is democratic, the rest of the Middle East will be democratic. A transformed Middle East—if it takes—will free millions of people from bondage under the thumbs of dictators, dampen Muslim fundamentalism, and guarantee continued U.S. access to vital oil resources, so it's worth it—even if a few thousand

Americans and many thousands of Iraqis die in the process."

OR

- "We used despicable means to imprison thousands of sometimes innocent people and systematically subject them to abuse and torture ranging all the way up to death. Still, we had to do it, because if even one of them coughed up critical intelligence about Al Qaeda before expiring, it would make all the other poor Muslim people's ruined lives worth the cost."

All this bobbing and weaving would be rendered completely unnecessary if you could make a fair, honest case for going to Iraq. Thing is, it's tough. Threads of logic get all tangled up until they are inextricable. It was easier to conflate—to invent—a connection between Saddam Hussein and Al Qaeda, to exaggerate or even falsify evidence of WMD. "Well, the public won't really understand the complex reasons we must invade Iraq. Public won't buy it. It's too complicated for them. It would take too much time. People have old-fashioned ideas about wars being waged for self-defense only."

Modern conservative leaders, riding on the heels of Bush and Karl Rove, believe they were nursing an ailing empire back to health by baring fangs. Journalists and citizens were naive; they could sit back and observe, but there would be no participation.

Political theorist and linguist George Lakoff argues that modern conservatism likes to use a "stern father" model as the core of its philosophy of governance. In this rhetorical system, conservatives see government as a strong, dominant "father." Dad's job, therefore, is to make sure that his kids—also known as American citizens—are disciplined into adults who are fiscally and morally responsible. Funny—that sounds an awful lot like the theory of British monarchical rule at which Locke took such offense more than three hundred years ago.

It's also precisely the sort of worldview that leads to a "father knows best" approach to public affairs, including useful white lies (Santa Claus/WMD), pervasive secrecy (the stack of *Penthouse* magazines in the sock drawer/presidential privilege), and physical discipline (the belt/"extraordinary rendition").

Through acts like these, modern conservatism has eaten away at its own moral core, a core that has been present in one form or another since Patrick Henry and Thomas Jefferson stood up and challenged the rising power of the federal government in the name of states' and individuals' rights.

Hawkish author Tom Clancy had a chance to talk to Richard Perle about the Iraq war, and he got a firsthand opportunity to hear the grinding gears of neoconservative logic.

"He was saying how Colin Powell was being a wuss because he was overly concerned with the lives of the troops," Clancy told the Associated Press in 2004. "And I said, 'Look . . . he's supposed to think that way!' And Perle didn't agree with me on that. People like that worry me."[46]

In 1757, Washington—like Powell, a well-known "wuss"—wrote a long, angry letter to the lieutenant governor of colonial Virginia, Brit Robert Dinwiddie. Washington was outraged about the miserable condition of his troops, who were being used as cannon fodder by an imperial power that refused to grant them political rights.

Washington's passion about ragged uniforms, poor equipment,

and hideous fighting conditions came from having to put together a pragmatic worldview based on battlefield experience and frontier living, not conferences at the American Enterprise Institute and the University of Chicago. Washington, like most soldiers with war experience, hated to see people sacrificed to the bayonet and cannon. He wept for fallen troops.

Perle, like the rest of the neoconservative architects of the Iraq conflict, had never experienced anything rougher than the occasional shouting match with a war widow, and was eager to send young Americans into harm's way in the name of a secret ideal.

While conservatives accuse progressives of moral relativism, the truth is that the moral relativists in the house are the conservatives themselves. The ease with which conservative figures such as Roy Blunt, Tom DeLay, William Bennett, Karl Rove, and many others have brushed off the human consequences of their policies and skated through controversy is testimony to how "being a conservative" inevitably ranks above morality and decency, most notably at the government's highest levels.

The rules bend like hot rubber when a Republican is indicted.

Progressives talk about human rights and about transparent government.

Conservative commentators describe torture as a useful tool, how some civil rights need to be sacrificed on the altar of "national security," and how the people shouldn't be allowed to know what the people's government is up to—for "security reasons."

Morality is, of course, inextricably tied to religious faith. Morality and religion, some would suggest, are just two threads of the same rope—the more religiously passionate one is, the more fully moral one has become.

By conflating the two, you could quickly conclude that the Bush administration, with its faith-based programs and Bible-quoting figurehead, is the most moral since the country's establishment. This is no accident. Karl Rove, Frank Luntz, Dick Cheney—not the world's most observant and churchgoing folks—cynically understand the power of Christian morality. Images that invoke the power resonate like few others. They get things done. And to Bush and friends, getting things done, by any means necessary, is the key.

But this is where the Founding Fathers would disagree. Like most of their peers in the Enlightenment, the Founding Fathers generally divorced morality and proclamation of religious faith from each other. Benjamin Franklin observed:

> *I think all the heretics I have known have been virtuous men. They have the virtue of fortitude, or they could not venture to own their heresy; and they cannot afford to be deficient in any of the other virtues, as that would give advantage to their many enemies; and they have not, like orthodox sinners, such a number of friends to excuse or justify them.*[47]

CARTHAGO DELENDA EST

Let's pretend for a moment that Rome was New York and its political and economic rival Carthage was Boston. In this situation, the phrase *Carthago delenda est* would be the equivalent of saying, "The Red Sox suck"—or more accurately, "The Red Sox suck, and let's burn Boston to the ground, and salt all the surrounding fields so that nothing ever grows there again, and also destroy all the *Cheers* DVD box sets."

The literal translation of the phrase is "Carthage must be destroyed," and it gives you a good idea of the ambitions of the Roman senator Marcus Cato. He wasn't interested in humbling the city of Carthage, or swaying it with diplomacy, or even neutering it militarily. It had to be wiped off the face of the earth. This tendency toward vengeance—or its opposing virtue, compassion—is a telling trait in a politician or political party.

In the wake of their victory against the hated British forces in the Revolutionary War, the Founding Fathers had many opportunities for sweet revenge against British prisoners, against Tory sympathizers and merchants, and even against members of their own faction who disagreed with the new "party line." In fact, most revolutions have followed a similar pattern of fraternity, revolution, insecurity, and bloodshed. It would have surprised no one if the American Revolution had concluded in a similar fashion.

But the Founders preferred, overwhelmingly, pragmatic and (mostly) morally wholesome mercy. About the forfeiture of British property and debt and the treatment of Tories, Jefferson wrote: "It may be mentioned as proof both of the lenity of our government and unanimity of its inhabitants, that though this war has now raged near seven years, not a single execution for treason has taken place."

Alexander Hamilton's father-in-law, Philip Schuyler, exhibited some of the most remarkable chivalry of the war. In 1777, the British general John Burgoyne burned down Schuyler's house and most of his other buildings during the battle of Saratoga. After the British defeat and Burgoyne's surrender, Schuyler had the destroyer of his property at his mercy. So he lined up Schuyler and his twenty-person entourage . . . and invited them to stay in the Schuyler mansion in Albany. There, he wreaked further vengeance upon them by feeding them delicious dinners.

What a lily-livered liberal. Had they been contemporaneously fashionable, he probably would have offered them "understanding and therapy, too."

Hamilton himself was noted for his merciful spirit. In his biography of the Founder, Ron Chernow writes:

> *Hamilton was exemplary in his treatment of the enemy. Some of his men clamored for revenge against the captives [after the siege of Yorktown], and one captain was about to run a British officer through the chest with a bayonet when Hamilton interceded to prevent any bloodshed. He later reported proudly, "Incapable of imitating examples of barbarity and forgettting recent provocations, the soldiers spared every man who ceased to resist."*[48]

After the war, Hamilton would go on to defend British Loyalists in court; though the Tories' cause was lost, Hamilton was determined that they not also lose their properties and futures in the newly united states. He was similarly sympathetic to the plight of Native Americans, warning New York governor George Clinton about the importance of maintaining good relations with the tribes, and championing humane reconciliation over continued bloodshed.

A similar spirit can be noted in the personal correspondence between Jefferson and Adams, who often fought bitterly over political questions. Jefferson noted that even Adams's political enemies would concede his honesty and decency, and, in 1791, he worked hard to mend his friendship with his political sparring partner.

"That you and I differ in our ideas of the best form of government is well known to us both," wrote Jefferson, "but we have differed as friends should do, respecting the purity of each other's motives." In a letter to his grandson Thomas Jefferson Randolph, Jefferson cited Franklin's rules for civilized disputes—"never to contradict any body." If urged to state an opinion, Franklin suggested, do it through asking questions, or by suggesting doubts.

This isn't to paper over the fact that the Founders (particularly Jefferson and Hamilton) sometimes engaged in wicked dogfights with one another. They did. But even the worst political rivalries didn't come down to deadly force; the one glaring exception, the duel between Burr and Hamilton, stands out for how atypical it was.

George Washington, for his part, was no fan of factions or political witch hunts. Far from working toward the destruction of any one individual or political party, Washington was interested in building—through personal leadership and example—the executive branch of the newly founded federal government, and guiding the country through the series of crises he would face over the years of his presidency. A single-party system, in fact, would be akin to the kind of repressive government Americans were trying to avoid. These days, it is an open ambition of some members of Bush's inner circle.

At a time when fundamentalist terrorism is viewed as the archenemy of modern American democracy, Superman Karl Rove—the undisputed architect of the modern Bush political machine—famously said, during a June 2005 speech to the New York state Conservative Party:

> *Conservatives saw the savagery of 9/11 and the attacks and prepared for war. Liberals saw the savagery of the 9/11 attacks and wanted to prepare indictments and offer therapy and understanding for our attackers.*

The degree to which the Bush administration's Supermen have ascended and to which their *Carthago delenda est* attitude has become the party line can be observed in the modern Republican Party's zeal for changing the playing field—redistricting in order to create invincible Republican legislative majorities, preventing labor unions from contributing to politicians to support their own interests, and suppressing the black (and/or poor) vote however humanly possible.

It can also be observed from the fervor with which "enemies of the party"—Democrats, whistleblowers, plain speakers, honest public servants who do their job when it's politically inconvenient to the party—get bounced out of their jobs and slandered by Scott McClellan during the presidential briefing. Richard Clarke's transformation from rock-solid professional on the front lines of the war on terror into "partisan Democrat with a book to sell" was instantaneous.

SUPERMEN'S SECRET WEAPON

Now let's give it up for fear for a moment. It totally works. Despots from Stalin through Castro have learned the effectiveness of a good hard whack to the knuckles for those who diverge from the party line. In fact, it's absolutely naive to think that you can run a government without horse-trading and whip-cracking. But it's another thing entirely to make the humiliation and eradication of the only other major political party a point of pride.

On a grand scale, the war on the Democratic Party's traditional pillars of financial support—including unions, lawyers, and Jewish

Americans—has been prosecuted with a sort of strategtic ruthlessness that would make Machiavelli proud. The plan, in short: Stop unions from being able to contribute dues to political campaigns. Use "tort reform" as a way to make it impossible for citizens to hold corporations accountable (see the long-awaited *Exxon Valdez* payments to the out-of-work fishermen on Prince William Sound). And equate Ariel Sharon with Likud with Israel with Jews and then back Sharon's often destructive policies to the hilt.

All of these plans, politically inspired as they may be, have negative consequences for Americans in general. The attempt to castrate unions puts still more power into the hands of large corporations increasingly answerable only to the bottom line—not to consumers, or their own employees. "Tort reform" lets corporations calculate the exact financial cost of releasing unsafe (or fatal) products onto the market, thereby endangering the public. And the unblinking support of Sharon has written a blank check for a series of outrageous abuses in the Gaza Strip and West Bank that guarantee a continuation of the Palestinian–Israeli conflict for generations to come.

On a small scale, the outing of Valerie Plame's identity in order to punish her husband—a well-informed and responsible critic of a poorly planned and irresponsible war—is indicative of the "out for blood" mentality that has caused this administration much well-deserved heartburn. The fact that Plame wasn't even the political opponent in question but, instead, that opponent's wife, gives even more evidence of the length that administration goons are willing to go to in order to annihilate "enemies."

Wilson could have been treated with silence, or his charge could have simply been papered over with more lies—they were cheap and plentiful at the time he wrote his *New York Times* op-ed casting doubt on a key piece of evidence pertaining to Iraq's awe-inspiring WMD program.

Instead, Rove and company went for the jugular—a ruthless and stupid reaction that led to the indictment of Scooter Libby on five assorted counts, and the continuing (as of this writing) investigation of Rove himself.

The story of Tony Sanchez is also illuminating. A rags-to-riches success story in the Texas oil and banking industries, Sanchez donated $300,000 to Bush's campaign for governor—making him one of the president's leading Democratic supporters. Sanchez also backed Bush's run for reelection, and his run for president.

In 2002 Sanchez jumped into politics himself, challenging Rick Perry, and hoping his past support of the president might lead Bush to stay his hand against his old friend. To quote Paul Begala, writing in the September 2004 edition of *Washington Monthly*:

> *Fat chance.*
>
> *Bush not only actively campaigned for Perry, but he also allowed Perry's goons to run vicious ads against Sanchez. They portrayed Sanchez as somehow complicit in the 1985 torture and murder of DEA agent Kiki Camarena because during the 1980s, drug dealers used Sanchez's bank (as they did most banks on the border) without his knowledge.*
>
> *What the ads did not mention is that Sanchez helped federal authorities bust the bad guys, and earned the praise of the Reagan Justice Department. In fact, when the ads ran, David Almaraz, the DOJ official who handled the investigation, denounced them, saying, "Perry's claim is ab-*

solutely preposterous and completely false, without any foundation and fact."

Sanchez, of course, got crushed. Ditto war veteran Senators John McCain and Max Cleland, who both fell victim to some of the nastiest slander campaigns in recent memory. Cleland, a disabled veteran, was a particularly ironic victim—he'd crossed the aisles to back the president on his tax cuts and the war in Iraq. That wasn't good enough. His patriotism was smeared in a vicious series of ads that featured photos of Cleland, Saddam Hussein, and Osama bin Laden.

Go back to the Founding Fathers to see why a vicious "scorched earth" policy is the wrong way to conduct politics within your own borders. Or you can go all the way back to Sun Tzu, who wrote that while it's good to win a war, it's better to let your enemies fight among themselves—and it's best of all to not have any enemies at all.

But nobody in the White House is consulting *The Art of War*. And it's clear that no one is looking to the Founders for guidance.

SEPTEMBER 25, 2002

Bush: Saddam, Al Qaeda Ties "Don't Make Sense"

WASHINGTON, D.C.—President George W. Bush reacted publicly today for the first time to reports that Al Qaeda agents have established ties to Iraqi intelligence. The claim, if true, would be a major plank in the platform of pro-war neoconservatives, who suggest that Iraqi WMD and an alliance with Islamist terrorists constitute an immediate threat to the safety of the United States.

"I've looked at this evidence," said the president, "and, frankly, I do not find it to be compelling."

To the surprise of many observers, Bush cited the example of America's first president when describing his methodology for assessing the evidence.

"One of the things I admired about George Washington was that he always gathered all the evidence he could before making a decision. I'm no Washington, but I'm trying to follow in his footsteps. I read everything I could lay my hands on about Iraq and Al Qaeda. Talked to journalists who'd met Hussein. Phoned up people in the region, professors at universities all over the world. Everyone kept saying: Al Qaeda hates this guy. And Saddam knows that militant Islamists like Al Qaeda are the biggest threat to his rule after the Kurds and Shiites. Last thing he wants to do is give 'em a bomb. They'd light up Baghdad or Riyadh before trying to haul it to DC or New York."

The president promised to direct at least nominal intelligence resources toward the question of Iraqi WMD and Al Qaeda ties, but said, "There are more pressing problems—the rise of militant Islam is a global problem, and it needs to be fought with active intelligence work. We can't spare these people to pursue far-fetched conspiracy theories."

Critics have hailed the president's pragmatic approach to intelligence gathering, described by many as being driven by the facts and not conservative ideology. The president explicitly described his reasoning during an interview last week where he said: "The facts come first, and I'm interested in getting results we can trust. That's why I overruled the Army decision to fire more than twenty gay Arab and Farsi linguists. That was just nuts. Don't people realize there's a war on?"

SEVEN

BUILDING A NATION, SCRIPTING A WAR

My secret opinion has ever been, and still is, that God Almighty will not give up a people to military destruction, or leave them unsupportedly to perish, who had so earnestly and so repeatedly sought to avoid the calamities of war, by every decent method which wisdom could invent.

—Thomas Paine, *The Crisis,* December 23, 1776

Intelligence gathered by this and other governments leaves no doubt that the Iraq regime continues to possess and conceal some of the most lethal weapons ever devised.

—President Bush, remarks to the nation, March 17, 2003

B Y THE TIME the thirteen American colonies finally made war on their imperial master in 1775, they had reached the end of a long road. Economically, British taxes had enfeebled and enraged American merchants. Politically, taxation without representation had served as an irritant for decades. It didn't help that those tax revenues funded an occupation force that often abused colonists. And culturally, the increasingly self-reliant and populist Americans were growing more and more distant from their former kinsfolk across the Atlantic. They began to feel as if they belonged to a different country.

The storm of revolution brewed slowly, having been fed by decades of debate, agitation, provocation, and political organization. Its foremost proponents risked their own lives and fortunes to fight for a cause they truly believed in.

By the time the Bush administration led the country to war against the regime of Saddam Hussein in 2003, on the other hand, the prime architects of that war had reached the end of a short and expertly conducted campaign of fear-by-public-relations that had left most Americans (and journalists) convinced of the certain connection between Al Qaeda and Saddam Hussein.

The buildup to the Iraq war happened quickly, and mostly in secret, nourished by think tanks such as the American Enterprise Institute and academics who had been piped in directly from the University of Chicago into high-ranking Defense Department posts. Its foremost proponents risked only their reputations to start a war they thought to be a pretty good idea at the time.

The march to revolution—and an independent United States—contrasts markedly with the invasion of Iraq in all facets; and when stacked side by side, these two initiatives, while qualitatively dissimilar, still underscore vastly differing attitudes about collective decision-making, the relationship between leaders and average citizens, and the value of human life.

The Slow Walk to War

During the French and Indian War and Pontiac's Rebellion (in 1754–1763 and 1763, respectively), the British empire began shifting more of the cost of defending the colonies against "hostile" Indians onto the shoulders of its less-than-pleased colonists.

British forces began using open-ended search warrants to crack down on colonists evading the heavy regulation of the Navigation Acts. In 1761, a Massachusetts lawyer, James Otis, challenged the warrants in court. He argued that they violated the rights of the colonists.

Although Otis lost, John Adams would later write: "American independence was then and there born."

The conflict with Britain would take fourteen years to reach a head at the battles of Lexington and Concord. In the intervening years, colonists vigorously debated among themselves as citizens and equals about the intelligent course to pursue in the burgeoning conflict with the king.

In 1763, the fiery lawyer Patrick Henry argued in court that "a King, by disallowing Acts of this salutary nature, from being the father of his people, degenerated into a Tyrant and forfeits all right to his subjects' obedience."

Loyalists took up the opposing side, arguing that the revolution heralded a dangerous descent into mob rule and a postwar economic collapse. Even among would-be revolutionaries, there was hesitation; war was a dangerous choice, and not one to be made lightly. War, they warned, is no picnic, especially when it's waged in your backyard. Crops are burned. Civilians are killed. Wives and daughters are often raped. Houses are burned down, trade comes to a halt, and the most promising young men are put into disease-ridden camps or killed on the battlefield. These were powerful arguments, and they were taken into account.

Eventually, however, the compounded humiliations and economic pressures took their toll, and the M-80 of revolution was ignited in Britain's mailbox by the political Zippo that was Tom Paine's *Common Sense,* which, in clear and inflammatory language, made the case that a split with Britain was a moral and a political imperative. The small tract catalyzed much of the revolutionary consensus that was already building among the American colonists.

More important than a catchy argument, however, was the fact that the war was strategically feasible. As George Washington pointed out, the British would have to command and supply their forces across the Atlantic, whereas colonial forces would be defending areas near their own homes; colonial forces were simply much cheaper to maintain and easier to field.

The American forces were also better positioned to fight a long conflict. The longer the British remained in the field, the more political opposition to their troops would rise among the governed. The longer the American forces remained in the field, the more they would gain in training and come to resemble a real army—and perfect the irregular, insurgent style of fighting that would allow them to even the odds with a professional imperial army.

After some initial missteps, Washington would have the strategic intelligence to realize that his goal wasn't to tackle the entire British army—it was to wear away at its fringes, keep the Continental Congress and Continental Army in play, and run down the clock.

That—along with earnest and frequent consultations with a host of intelligent military and political advisers and the informed consent and participation of the American colonists—would win the day for the American cause.

HOUSTON'S WAR

Roughly a year and a half elapsed between September 11, 2001, and the invasion of Iraq. Few high-profile Americans—politicians or journalists—were willing to speak out against the seemingly inevitable tide of war for fear of getting steamrollered or ridiculed. The experts, nerdy professors with actual knowledge of Middle Eastern politics, and journalists who knew that Iraq without Saddam was an ethnic/religious time bomb, were shunted to the side, where they shared their wisdom with the readers of *Harper's, The New Yorker,* and *The New York Review of Books.* In their stead were lefty celebrities, invited to Fox news programs to engage in debates for which they weren't exactly prepared.

Although the 9/11 attack took place in Manhattan, this wasn't New York's war—it was Houston's. Houston wasn't listening to the academics and other area experts who knew the dangers and reasons for skepticism about the flimsy evidence that indicted Saddam as a nuke-packing Osama lover.

The men responsible for pushing the American colonies toward violent revolution met in taverns and farmhouses, and argued their tactics and strategies with the people whose lives were at stake. Of course, they could do that back then. But it's not the literal action that is instructive but the impulse. They abhorred the idea of war, but they eventually decided—collectively, galvanized by passionate but reasoned rhetoric and outrages like the Boston Massacre—that it was the only option.

The men and women responsible for pushing America toward war in Iraq used sales principles, pitching the war like a carnival huckster. Liberal use of fearful if false imagery and dire warnings combined with a cowering Congress led to a sale. The executive branch designed by the Framers would have been reluctant to go to war. A reluctant executive branch would have played down the evidence and tried to find ways to avoid the fight; it would rigorously have nailed down every piece of evidence hoping to disprove it, hoping to discover that it didn't hold water. But an executive branch spoiling for a fight would string together verbal bombs such as:

- "It's been pretty well confirmed that [Atta] did go to Prague and he did meet with a senior official of the Iraqi intelligence service in Czechoslovakia last April, several months before the attack."

  —Dick Cheney on NBC's *Meet the Press,* December 9, 2001, falsely linking Iraq to the 9/11 attacks

- "The British government has learned that Saddam Hussein recently sought significant quantities of uranium from Africa."

  —President Bush, in the State of the Union address, January 28, 2003 (a claim already disproved by the CIA before the speech)

- "We know that Saddam has the infrastructure, nuclear scientists to make a nuclear weapon. . . . We don't want the smoking gun to be a mushroom cloud."

  —Condoleezza Rice speaking to CNN's Wolf Blitzer, September 8, 2002

When chief UN weapons inspector Hans Blix cited a lack of "smoking guns," White House press secretary Ari Fleischer offered this assessment: "The problem with guns that are hidden is you can't see their smoke." Rather than the measured public voice of an administration that feared the bloodshed associated with war, that resisted armed conflict, that agonized over every possible option to war, this is the voice of an administration gleefully cruising to war on an out-of-control bobsled.

Unfortunately, the strategic foresight of the Bush team is also in direct contrast to and in violation of Framer principles. That foresight seems to have consisted of three steps:

STEP 1: Invade Iraq.

STEP 2: ???

STEP 3: Democracy!*

When attacking the rationale and the conduct of the Iraq war, critics tend to focus on tactical mistakes, such as canning most of the Iraqi army. Or letting looters play merry hell in the days after Saddam's overthrow. Or not invading with enough troops because Rumsfeld was determined to try out his cool new military doctrine. Or leaving giant piles of weapons and explosives lying around the country for insurgents to Hoover up and dump upon the heads of unsuspecting Marines and Iraqi government officials.

These were not, in fact, smart things to do.

*As adapted from the *South Park* episode "Gnomes (Underpants Gnomes)," first aired on December 16, 1998. The original Underpants Gnome plan for success: "Phase 1. Collect underpants. Phase 2. ??? Phase 3. PROFIT!"

But George Washington made tactical mistakes, too. Most memorably, a military disaster in New York, caused by Washington's bullheaded insistence on confrontation, nearly sank the Revolutionary War effort.

But the real problem with Iraq lies on the strategic level. Victory in Iraq, vaguely described as creating a stable democracy, is hard to measure, and it's not clear if a workable plan for accomplishing it was ever put in place before the invasion.

Moreover, the proposed democratic structure currently on the table seems to revolve around "Iraqis" working together to elect stable governments. But there are few "Iraqis," per se—most Iraqis identify first as Sunnis, or Shiites, or Kurds. The few Iraqis for whom the fires of nationalism truly burn are mostly former Baathists who liked the way Saddam brought everybody together under one iron fist.

The Bush administration also made a strategic miscalculation— or simply chose not to bother calculating at all, depending upon whom you ask—about the effect of the Iraq war on terrorism, and it's obvious. The Iraq conflict, with its piles of civilian casualties and unsettlingly credible accusations of torture by American forces, has proven to be the world's best recruiting poster for anti-American terrorists. This could have been anticipated, and, in fact, it was anticipated by Middle East experts, antiterrorism experts, CIA field agents, journalists with experience in the region, and a lot of people with heightened common sense. But they never got a chance to brief the president, even the antiterrorism experts and CIA field agents.

Bush's small, elite circle of loyalists choked off the flow of possibly negative or upsetting information about the upcoming invasion, anything that would take the plan for invasion off the rails, even if temporarily. And they choked off the flow of post-invasion commentary about how to fix the situation—or at least bring it to a mercifully swift closure.

Congressman Jack Murtha, a veteran who had supported the invasion of Iraq, became, in 2005, one of the first members of Congress to call for a clear plan for the withdrawal of American troops from Iraq. It was a bitter moment for the Vietnam War hero.

"Our troops have become the primary target of the insurgency," he said at a press conference, at one point in tears. "We have become a catalyst for violence. . . . It's time to bring [the troops] home."

Hilariously, after Murtha's press conference, a White House spokesman compared the hawkish Democrat to Michael Moore. Further, he suggested that Murtha, who had led the drive into Iraq in 1991 and who had supported most of the second Iraq war, was part of the "extreme liberal wing of the Democratic Party."[49]

This proved not to be the best tactic for the White House. The vet is as hawkish as they come, from either party. Making things worse, Vice President Dick Cheney foolishly got into the game. Cheney, who has never served a day in the military and who has a notorious credibility problem with those in uniform, had actually sought Murtha out in 1989. President George H. W. Bush asked Cheney to serve as the secretary of defense. Having little knowledge of military matters, Cheney begged Murtha for help. *The Nation* reported in 2005 that Cheney told Murtha: "I don't know a blankety-blank thing about defense."

Murtha did help him. But when Murtha made his comments about a plan for withdrawal from Iraq, Cheney ran the Sunday talk-show circuit like a Jet priming for a fight with a Shark—except the Jet had absolutely no street cred. "Some of the most irresponsible comments have, of course, come from politicians who actually voted in favor of authorizing force against Saddam Hussein."

Further, Cheney launched this bomb: "The president and I cannot prevent certain politicians from losing their memory, or their backbone—but we're not going to sit by and let them rewrite history."

"I like that," Murtha said when asked about Cheney's comments. "I like guys who've never been there that criticize us who've been there. I like that. I like guys who got five deferments and never been there and send people to war and then don't like to hear suggestions about what needs to be done."

President Bush finally engaged in damage control, calling Murtha a "fine man . . . who served our country with honor." He did not, however, personally contact Murtha to talk things over.

Where George Washington listened, Bush cuts off debate. A former senior member of the Coalition Provisional Authority in Baghdad observed the president consulting with top advisers.

> *The president would ask the generals, "Do you have what you need to complete the mission?" as opposed to saying, "Tell me, General, what do you need to win?" which would have opened up a whole new set of conversations. It just prevented the discussion from heading in a direction that would open up a possibility that we need more troops.*[50]

On the other hand, George Washington and his peers opened every door they could find looking for a way to avoid war. And when they found themselves forced to walk through it, they consulted some of the country's brightest minds not only for the way to win the fight, but for the way to build a new and better country after the defeat of Great Britain.

For Bush, there was only one door available after 9/11: the one marked "Invade Iraq."

From a profoundly pragmatic approach to war, America has moved to an approach that is profoundly utopian. American servicemen and women—and Iraqi civilians—are paying the price for an elite's personal pursuit of something called "complete victory."

Bush Press Conference

BUSH: I believe in the Bible. Love the Bible. And I think it's a beautiful book, a book we can all learn from. But the Bible's got some problems. What I've done . . . this is pretty cool, see . . . I've edited my Bible. See . . . get a shot of this. . . .

[Bush holds up a Bible with tattered pages covered in red ink. He flips through them casually, and little severed dog-ears of paper flutter onto the podium.]

BUSH: Went through the Gospels, and thought about them carefully. Kept the parts where Jesus—an amazing philosopher, my favorite philosopher, in fact—shares his thoughts on ethics and morality. And I just cut out the rest of the crap. The dogma, the superstition—yeah, wasn't feeling it. Just junked it. Now it's a lot purer. You historian types might want to call it the "Bush Bible," but I just like to call it Bible 2.0. Questions? Yes, the gentleman from *Christianity Today*.

Q: How long do you think it'll be before God strikes you down? Hours or days?

BUSH: I see what you mean, but I reject the basis of that question. God . . . you see, God's not a guy, with a beard, who throws lightning bolts at people when they question Christian dogma or Republican Party policy. Dogma's not sacred. Human life is sacred. And that's why I'm continuing my fight against abortion, pardoning all criminals on death row, ending the war in Iraq, and calling for Congress to restore all the benefits we've cut to the poorest and most vulnerable among us. Consistency is key, I find.

[A single massive strike of electricity arcs from the center of a perfectly blue sky to the podium's metal microphone, incinerating the president. A voice booms out from the sky.]

GOD: Don't let this happen again, folks. Your firstborn are counting on you.

EIGHT

PRESIDENT JESUS

*When you turn your heart and your life over to Christ,
when you accept Christ as the savior, it changes your heart.*
—George W. Bush, December 13, 1999[51]

Jesus to Bush: Stop using me as a reference.
—Bumper sticker

THE BIBLE IS ONE of humanity's most remarkable achievements. To spend time within its pages is to experience one of the most complicated, subtle, internally contradictory, and passionately moving works of art in the history of literature itself. There are some who argue that a superintelligent, all-seeing, all-knowing higher power, not a sometimes squabbling group of Middle Eastern mystics, is the actual author of the Old and New Testaments.

Okay.

That said, any objective reader who has spent more than a few unsupervised hours reading the Bible's schizophrenic litany of compassion, genocide, ethics, mysticism, prophecy, decency, morality, barbarism, and metaphor comes away with the hunch that there may have been *just a little* human effort involved in the book's composition. This is a stance that Bible scholars take on the Bible's authorship.

As unpopular as this view might be in Bush's America, as radical and iconoclastic a belief as it might seem today, where some segments of the population believe Bibles can stop bullets, this theory of the Bible was the standard viewpoint of the Founding Fathers, who considered the Good Book a flawed amalgam of spiritual wisdom, morality, dogma, and superstition, at best, or, at worst, an antiquated pile of rubbish best consigned to the trash bin of history.

In fact, Thomas Jefferson thought the Bible sufficiently flawed to actually edit his own version of the Good Book, something that the Christian Coalition would Not Approve Of. Not only was Jefferson patently dissatisfied with the Bible, he never even claimed to cite Jesus as a primary influence, which is basically a prerequisite for aspiring politicians today.

In a letter Jefferson wrote from Paris on February 15, 1789, he talked about his real heroes:

> *With respect to the busts & pictures I will put off till my return from America all of them except Bacon, Locke and Newton, whose pictures I will trouble you to have copied for me . . . I consider them as the three greatest men that have ever lived, without any exception.*[52]

"What Would Bacon Do?" seems like an unlikely slogan for a world leader, but it makes considerably more sense than its "force beats facts" alternative, "What Would Dobson Do?"

Jefferson, like most of his Enlightenment contemporaries, just didn't buy the supernatural stories and churchy dogma that infused Christianity with a sort of you're-going-to-hell vibe.

Here's Jefferson again, in a letter he sent in 1823 to John Adams, commenting on the divine nature of Jesus:

> *The day will come when the mystical generation of Jesus, by the supreme being as his father in the womb of a virgin will be classed with the fable of the generation of Minerva in the brain of Jupiter.*

That's a downright impeachable thought these days. And we should all be more than a little worried that a bunch of guys without central heating, the Internet, or the benefit of modern dentistry were this much more pragmatic—and radically progressive—than their modern-day counterparts.

But Thomas Paine makes Jefferson's Bible-editing look like child's play: Paine thought the whole book was a cauldron of wickedness and advocated its swift transportation to Ye Olde Landfill. He wraps up *Common Sense* with an address to the Quakers:

> *Sincerely wishing, that as men and Christians, ye may always fully and uninterruptedly enjoy every civil and religious right; and be, in your turn, the means of securing it to others; but that the example which ye have unwisely set, of mingling religion with politics,* may be disavowed and reprobated by every inhabitant of America *[emphasis mine].*

Paine was a passionate believer—in freedom, in individual rights, and, yes, in God. The muse of the Declaration of Independence, the true believer who risked his life during the

French Revolution, was a Believer. He just thought that human-made institutions distorted the Big Guy's true intentions.

What gives?

Were Paine and Jefferson out of step with their supergodly peers? Maybe a little schizophrenic, confused, rebellious without causes?

Not in the least. Alexander Hamilton wanted to marry a woman "with a moderate streak of religion."[53] (He in fact married the very pious Elizabeth Schuyler, but regularly failed to make it to church himself.) Benjamin Franklin was chased from Boston as a young man in 1723 after Hub residents labeled him an "atheist" and an "infidel."[54] Franklin also wrote in his autobiography of the emptiness of being "saved" if such salvation isn't accompanied by good works toward fellow human beings. And here's George Washington in a 1784 letter to his aide Tench Tilghman, describing the kind of workers he wanted to hire for the renovation of Mount Vernon:

> If they are good workmen, they may be of Assia, Africa, or Europe. They may be Mahometans, Jews, or Christian of any sect—or they may be Atheists—I would however prefer middle aged to young men and those who have good countenances & good characters on ship board, to others who have nether of these to recommend them—although, after all, the proof of the pudding must be in the eating.[55]

As usual, Washington the pragmatist. Why let religion interfere with your having a top-quality patio? Or a clean, well-ordered government?

SAVING RELIGION FROM ITSELF

In their revolutionary vision, the Founders did not want religion erased from the face of the earth. There was no post-revolutionary backlash against churches as there was in France, or as there would be in early-twentieth-century Russia. Even the most radical Founders harbored a deep respect for religion as a private force, that bond between a person and his or her God, and as an organizing principle for community life.

They just didn't think it should be used to organize government. There were just too many complications. For example, a politician who invokes God or religion as a defense for a certain action he took cannot be adequately challenged on that defense. An opponent would certainly run the risk of being attacked as a heretic or a doubter. This is a risk few politicians are willing to take, and for good reason: in American politics, it's kind of hard to bounce back from being labeled an atheist.

When affairs of state are bound up with affairs of religion, the Founders reasoned, both suffer—religion, because it becomes a tool for ambitious and selfish men, and the state because charlatans can invoke "God's will" to silence their critics.

Saudi Arabia and Iran are just two countries that have attempted to integrate religion and state. The results have been less than inspiring: no free speech, lack of open debate, poor human rights records, and no democratic representation. Oh, and women murdered, by their own families, on suspicion of adultery.

The very subjective and somewhat paradoxical nature of the Bible and Christian dogma may be why none of the Framers found it reliable enough to use as a model for the Constitution—not with clearheaded mortals such as John Locke and David Hume cranking out the kind of organized liberal thought necessary to inspire the American nation.

NOT REALLY BIBLICAL

In not invoking the Christian God at any point throughout the Constitution, the Framers courted political disaster. As mentioned in earlier chapters, their a-religious approach and their decision to ban "religious tests" for officeholders provoked a firestorm of criticism from the era's Jerry Falwells, James Dobsons, and Ralph Reeds, who wanted a godly document that would reinforce Christian supremacy. Yale College president Reverend Timothy Dwight, for example, blasted the Constitution in 1812, saying: "The nation has offended Providence. We formed our Constitution without any acknowledgement of God; without any recognition of His mercies to us, as a people, of His government, or even of His existence. The [Constitutional] Convention, by which it was formed, never asked even once, His direction or His blessings, upon their labors."[56]

Whether they were devoted to God, or indifferent, the Framers were intensely distrustful of man's attempts, whether via scripture or organized religion, to turn any interpretation of God's will into a political force.

From that iconoclastic thinking, which set the stage for the Great Experiment, which largely has succeeded almost beyond measure, we've come to this: George W. Bush.

Ask George W. Bush to define himself in terms of his personal character, and he will tell you he is a born-again Christian. Ask George W. Bush what his guiding political principles are, and he will tell you he is a born-again Christian. When making decisions about whether or not to invade a country that has not made a first strike against us, George W. Bush will tell you he's a born-again Christian.

In fact, Christian dogma is the main motif of the Bush administration, and Christian passwords and catchphrases are the rhetorical tools of his political philosophy. His favorite philosopher plays double duty as his personal savior. His favorite book is the Bible. The New Testament is his spiritual home turf, and the philosophical stadium in which he fights his battles and celebrates his victories.

Consider the following tricks of the trade the Bush administration employs in its day-to-day business practices:

- the branding of "evildoers": consider Bush's "Axis of Evil" comments about Iraq, Iran, and North Korea;

- strict enforcement of personal loyalty: the importance of personal loyalty has been emphasized to the point that devotion to free thought and fair debate has been thrown into the shadows;

- the pampering of the rich and the abandonment of the poorest people to the mercies of "private charity" and "the free market."

If you were to break out the biblical scorecard and rate the above Bush principles, you would likely rate them, respectively: biblical, biblical, not really biblical. Or more specifically, Old Testament,

Old Testament, the exact opposite of the teachings of Jesus in the New Testament. (It is, admittedly, difficult to reconcile the two halves of the Holy Bible.*)

When you examine the Bush administration's track record from a theological perspective, it can sometimes appear that Bush is actually a Bible-hating apostate—at least going by some of his policy decisions. Of course, that isn't the case, but you can certainly argue it if you're in the right mood.

What is shocking is that Bush is dedicated to the worst Old Testament concepts of tribal loyalty and savage "eye for an eye" justice, the kind of things that even Old Testament fans are kind of embarrassed about. New Testament concepts of compassion, forgiveness, and tolerance are nowhere to be found in Bush's Rules of Order.

Bush kicked off his 2001 inauguration by having a Protestant evangelist minister officially dedicate the ceremony to Jesus Christ, whom the minister declared for all Americans watching the coverage to be "our savior." Billy Graham's son invoked "the Father, the Son, the Lord Jesus Christ" to bless the Bush presidency. And it's been a constant touchstone of public inspiration ever since. Christianity, the president said in 2001 at the National Prayer Breakfast, "has sustained me in moments of success and in moments of disappointment. Without it, I'd be a different person. And without it, I doubt I'd be here today."

---

*The Bible is, in many ways, ethically divided: the disconnect between the jealous, demanding, temperamental maniac that is Old Testament Yahweh, and the stern but loving ethicist that is New Testament Jesus.

WHAT WOULD PRESIDENT JESUS DO?

It isn't stretching things to assume that George W. Bush asks himself what Jesus would do in any given situation. He considers Jesus to be his personal savior, his intellectual and spiritual guide, his rock. In that spirit, let's posit a few rhetorical WWJD questions:

- Would Jesus, governor of the state of Texas, skim vacantly through appeals for clemency in record time, granting almost none, and leaving the rest to fry in the electric chair?

- Would candidate Jesus, running in the Republican primary against war hero John McCain, use push-polls to spread the word about McCain's alleged "illegitimate black child"—or would he publicly praise him for adopting a homeless Bangladeshi baby?

- Would President Jesus drive out members of his administration for following their consciences and label them as "disloyal" former employees? Or would he engage them in rational debate about their objections to state policy?

- Would President Jesus be unable, at a nationally televised press conference, to think of a single mistake he'd committed over the course of a disastrous first term, or would he humbly admit to having made many mistakes, and hope that, with God's help, his second term would be better for everyone?

- Would President Jesus hire and retain Karl Rove and Frank Luntz, the modern Machiavellian schemers whose skillful command of Orwellian rhetoric puts them at the top of the list for "Modern Americans Most Likely to Burn in the Eighth Circle of Hell"?*

- Would President Jesus use religion to bully his opponents, funnel public money to "faith-based" political supporters, suppress the effective fight against AIDS in Africa, and create a personal story as a "redeemed born-again Christian" after a life of indolence, greed, and failure, while backing that story up with indolence (most vacation days of any president in history), greed (Halliburton, anyone?), and failure?

The political philosopher Jean-Jacques Rousseau, in describing the ideal form of a government, spoke of the need for some sort of state religion to bind citizens together with their leaders, but also suggested that any true approximation of Christianity would be a mistake—a loving, forgiving, peaceful country would get eaten alive by its neighbors (see Tibet).

The point is not that President Bush and his administration's love of the Bible and of religion in general is a bad thing. Instead, the point is that the "Christianity" that Bush actually seems to in-

---

*For those of you rusty on your Dante, that's the final resting place for pimps, seducers, simonists, soothsayers, frivolous litigators, hypocrites, thieves, counselors of fraud in war, counselors of violence, and counterfeiters.

corporate into his public affairs is country-club Christianity—the Christianity of networking, of public piety and private vice, and of power helping power. And the "Bible" that seems to influence the administration's actions most transparently is the Bible of tribal loyalty and fierce, violent retribution—in short, the Really Bad Bits.

This is exactly the sort of politics-by-personal-interpretation-of-religion that the Founders hoped to see America transcend. "I have ever thought religion a concern purely between our God and our consciences," Jefferson wrote in 1816.[57]

Those words capture the spirit of his founding peers—and bring a fierce beat down upon the Bible-thumping corruption that has become the filthy-tasting Everlasting Gobstopper of modern American politics.

THE Alternate Universe DAILY SPECTATOR

June 5, 2004

In Wake of Torture Scandal, Heads Roll

WASHINGTON, D.C.—President Bush accepted yesterday the resignation of Defense Secretary Donald Rumsfeld for his role in the ongoing scandal surrounding the torture of detainees in Iraq's Abu Ghraib prison.

"I said while campaigning for the White House that this was going to be an administration where people were held accountable for their actions," Bush said during a press availability today. "And I meant it."

Rumsfeld offered his resignation as the magnitude of "Torturegate" became increasingly clear after a series of leaks and investigative reports by writers such as *The New Yorker*'s Seymour Hersh.

"This nation owes a debt of gratitude to Seymour Hersh and every one of his colleagues who followed up on this story," Bush said to a roomful of slightly stunned White House correspondents. "This story is something that's hurt America's reputation as a moral country around the world, and the only way we're going to rebuild that reputation is by cleaning house."

Bush went on to say that America's "soft power"—its strength projected through its culture, its leadership of international organizations, and its reputation for fairness and decency—was even greater than its "hard power" as measured in bullets and bombs.

Rumsfeld's resignation is already being hailed by pundits as a watershed moment for America's image abroad. Bush cited the way George Washington and company handled foreign affairs as inspiration for his "get-tough" policy regarding Torturegate.

"America's Founding Fathers saw Great Britain as a belligerent imperial power with no regard for international opinion or individual rights, that would torture and execute its enemies at will. That's the road we were headed down, and I didn't like it. So I took the steering wheel and turned this puppy around.

"That's leadership," he added. "You can work that into your headlines if you want. 'President promises, delivers leadership' has a very nice ring to it, in one man's opinion.

"That man is me, the president," he concluded, arms akimbo.

NINE

WE WERE THE WORLD

Mr. President, I fear that this administration is, perhaps unwittingly, heading us into a miserable cycle of waging wars that isolate our nation internationally and stir up greater hatred of America. . . . We owe it to the American people not to rush into a war.

—Senator Jim Jeffords, October 2002

Fuck Saddam, we're taking him out!

—George W. Bush, as quoted in *Time*, March 2002

LIKE THE FRENCH REVOLUTION, America's new Constitutional government was the physical embodiment of some of the Enlightenment's boldest ideas. But unlike the ultimately bloody mess in France, the American experiment was restrained by and refracted through the adapted institutions of the British Empire—and some worldly philosophers such as David Hume, John Locke, and the Baron de Montesquieu.

It was a government that was wary of government. It was a government that recognized the danger governments pose to the governed. It was a government of people who knew, firsthand, the horrors of war, and had little interest in experiencing them again.

In the centuries that have followed the American Revolution, this grand experiment has come to represent many things to people around the world, and not all of it is good. To Filipinos at the turn of the twentieth century, it meant colonial oppression. To most residents of the Soviet bloc, it meant neocolonialism and crude capitalist exploitation. To Iranians in 1979, it meant the rise of the Great Satan. And to its own black, Native American, and otherwise disenfranchised citizens, it represented oppression and prejudice.

But to many others, across the globe, America has long been a beacon of hope, a place where things actually worked, where power was peacefully transferred after elections, where you were free to speak your mind, worship however you pleased—or not even worship at all. America was free of corrupt politicians and courts, and it passed honest laws. You were free to earn shitloads of money, and give your kids a life happier and easier than your own. A model for your own country, if not a destination for you and your family.

World War II—and the farsighted Marshall Plan that followed in its wake—made America the natural focal point for those who believed that democracy and human rights were the wave of the future. Fascism was exposed for the cruel and exploitive sham that it was, and Communism was already well into its long and destructive slide into irrelevance.

And while cynical Cold War manipulations of developing nations—to say nothing of the Vietnam War and the bombing of Cambodia—took the bloom off the rose for many observers, America remained "the Leader of the Free World" in all meaningful ways right up until the year 2000.

The country's long turn in the spotlight stems, at least initially, from the pragmatism and humility of foreign policy as practiced by the Founding Fathers. Humble, in that, having just fought a long, destructive war against the world's greatest empire, America's first generation of leaders understood how important it was to carefully nurture their new country, lest another conflict wipe it from the face of the earth. Because we weren't always packing nukes. Pragmatic, in that personal grudges and short-term passions were considered poor guidelines for decision-making.

This pragmatism was demonstrated perhaps most dramatically when George Washington, Alexander Hamilton, and John Jay—then chief justice of the United States—successfully concluded the Treaty of London (the Jay Treaty) with Britain in 1795. Seen by nativists and many well-meaning patriots (such as Thomas Jefferson) as a sellout to a recently defeated but still venomous enemy, the Jay Treaty granted most-favored-nation trading status to Britain in return for British forces vacating western forts on American territory and compensating owners of ships seized by the British during the war of independence.

Impassioned public protests against the treaty featured little ditties like: "Damn John Jay! Damn everyone that won't damn John Jay! Damn everyone that won't put lights in his window and sit up all night damning John Jay!"

Although the Jay Treaty made a deal with an unpopular foreign power, it wasn't larded with personal grudges or ideology. Instead, it was agreed upon because of the domestic political boon it offered the young country, even if the freshly victorious and newly American citizens wanted to punish the British. It required a tremendous expenditure of political capital to accomplish. It required balls of steel.

By rubbing off some of the revolutionary grime that obscured America's window onto the world, Hamilton and Washington knew that trade with Britain—stimulated by a common language and shared commercial tradition—would be key to the nation's future in a way that trade with France or other European countries would not. It was the smart move, the pragmatic next step, the short-term pain for the long-term gain that characterized so many of the Framers' most important decisions.*

OF TREATIES AND TORTURE

Stop a conservative on the street and ask her about her views on the Constitution, and she'll probably tell you that she's an "originalist."

An "originalist" interpretation of the Constitution relies on two main points, which are supported in both the actual text and the contemporary subtext of the document.

The first is that treaties, once signed and ratified by the Senate, become the law of the land. As such, they're not to be casually disregarded or violated by anyone, even, or especially, the president.

This point was important to the Founding Fathers because of the power that European countries wielded over the still young and vulnerable republic. If a chief executive—who, after all, might only serve a single four-year term—could casually discard treaties, America would be put into a position where effective diplomacy would be much harder to conduct, and war far more likely.

Now, a believer in a living, evolving Constitution might say: "Hey! Times have changed. We should violate treaties away when-

---

*Today, we have seen a less practical approach to foreign policy; the Bush administration approach has been (kindly) characterized as "muscular unilateralism." Muscular unilateralism is an approach that uses the nation's military and economic muscles to unilaterally punch smaller countries in the kidneys when they disagree with American foreign policy.

ever we'd like, because we're the biggest, toughest kid on the planet."

But not an originalist. Not a conservative. A conservative would honor the Framers' intent.

And yet the Bush administration, that cabal of conservatism, has almost systematically violated international treaties. In his term as president, Bush has disregarded critical portions of the Geneva Conventions Protocol, the 1970 Nuclear Non-Proliferation Treaty, the Anti-Ballistic Missile Treaty, and the 1972 Biological and Toxin Weapons Convention, among others.

Therefore, the Bush administration should be credited as one of the most radical and nonconservative administrations in American history in terms of how it's handled the Constitution's legacy.

The second important originalist point is that Congress—not the president—holds the power to declare war. Even its right to devolve that right to the executive branch (as it did in the run-up to Iraq) is strongly questioned by serious constitutional scholars.

After Iraq, right-wing revisionists plumbed antique dictionaries in an attempt to suggest that while the Framers made a big deal about how Congress is the branch charged with the ability to—or allowed to—"declare" war, i.e., politely notify the enemy that hostilities are pending, they actually intended for the president to be able to arbitrarily *wage* war. It's pretty tidy. But it doesn't hold up upon further investigation. We'll get to that in a moment, once we've examined the administration's attitude about these two important points of originalist intent.

One of the best ways to do that is by studying the high-flying career of John Yoo. Deputy assistant attorney general until his resignation in 2003, John C. Yoo wasn't a brilliant jurist, or a champion of originalist intent. But he became vibrantly influential within the administration by Telling the President Exactly What He Wanted to Hear.

Imagined Dialogue Between George W. Bush and John C. Woo

BUSH: Okay, Mr. Yoo. I'd like to . . . well, break some international treaties about torture, and wage war unilaterally. Cool?

YOO: According to all my research, yes. Totally cool. According to the Constitution and this memo I've just cooked up, you have UNLIMITED POWER!

BUSH: Yes! I love the Constitution!

Yoo's personal best came in an August 2002 memorandum, in which he suggested that the president cannot be constitutionally barred from ordering torture during wartime. This suggestion stands in stark opposition, of course, to a treaty that the United States has signed and ratified, and a law passed by Congress in support of that treaty.

Yoo had been a member of the Federalist Society, a kind of perpetual bugbear on the topic of international law. It would be putting it politely to say, as Jane Mayer wrote in *The New Yorker,* that members of the Federalist Society "view international law with skepticism." September 11, Mayer wrote, gave Yoo an opportunity to implement some of his political ideas. "Soon after September 11th, Yoo and other Administration lawyers began advising President Bush that he did not have to comply with the Geneva Conventions in handling detainees in the war on terror."[58]

Throughout his tenure, Yoo proved himself the perfect go-to guy for making radical interpretations of the Constitution that granted gigawatts of previously unknown political power to the chief executive.

An executive who can make and break treaties at will, not to mention initiate war at will, is precisely the sort of executive branch that the Founding Fathers wanted to avoid. Why? Because that's the sort of leader that Britain had. He was called a king. In fact, the idea of a country that had just escaped the shackles of a monarchy allowing its executive royal powers was unthinkable. At the Constitutional Convention, Pierce Butler proposed giving the president the power to make war. Laughter ensued.

David Cole, writing in *The New York Review of Books* in 2005, noted that the vast majority of the delegates at the Constitutional Convention feared this sort of power in the hands of a chief executive. George Mason said the president was "not to be trusted" with powers of war and that those powers should be left with Congress as a way of "clogging rather than facilitating war."

Even Alexander Hamilton, the proponent of a strong (but not all-powerful) executive branch, said that "the Legislature alone can interrupt [the blessings of peace] by placing the nation in a state of war."

And yet John Yoo told *Frontline* that "the Constitution that we have gives a president a lot of power in wartime. The president is the commander in chief, and Congress writes statutes to try to give the president discretion to make the policies that will help win the war on terrorism." In addition, Yoo said that he thought the Justice Department had long believed Congress couldn't limit the commander in chief's power, "that Congress cannot tell the president how to exercise his judgment as commander in chief."

And so one can be forgiven if, knowing what the Founders intended and knowing the treachery they saw firsthand when power was vested too absolutely in the hands of a chief executive, she shudders upon recalling that after 9/11, John Yoo authored the first draft of the unprecedented war powers authorization granted to President Bush—which gave the president nearly unlimited power to fight the so-called war on terror, and that Congress passed that authorization "overwhelmingly."[59]

Further, Yoo's handiwork is all over the infamous "Bybee Memo," which sought ways around the Geneva Conventions to allow for the torture of "illegal combatants" in a quest for intelligence. According to *Frontline,* "Yoo claimed the U.S. ratification of the 1994 torture statute 'could be considered unconstitutional because it would interfere with the president's power as commander in chief.' . . . Taken in concert with the Congressional authorization passed on Sept. 14, 2001, which gave the president sweeping power to conduct the war on terror, and other recently released documents, the memos flesh out the Bush administration's expansive, and controversial, view of executive powers."[60]

Writing for *The Christian Science Monitor* in 2005, John Dillin interviewed Carol Berkin, professor of American history at City College of New York and Baruch College, for her take on what the Founders might have made of this mess. She said they had designated Congress—not the president—to be the heart of the federal government. "The president," Dillin wrote, "was supposed to be, well, more like an 'errand boy' for Congress."

"The public ranks Congress as successful, or not, depending on whether it enacts the president's program," Berkin told Dillin. Such an attitude would leave the Founding Fathers with "their mouths on the floor." Yet fighting against the president's program can be the political death knell for a member of Congress, especially if the party cuts off support in the next election.

The Framers had very different ideas on where the "errand boy" fit into the scheme of things.

John Adams believed that only a three-branched, oppositional government would work, and would be immune from corruption: two branches opposed to each other (legislative and executive) and one to balance them out.

James Madison wrote to Thomas Jefferson that "the constitution supposes, what the History of all Governments demonstrates, that the Executive is the branch of power most interested in war, and most prone to it. It has accordingly with studied care vested the question of war in the Legislature."

George Washington instructed his administration: "The Constitution vests the power of declaring war with Congress . . . therefore no offensive expedition of importance can be undertaken until after they have deliberated upon the subject, and authorized such a measure."

John Yoo wrote: "The Constitution that we have gives a president a lot of power in wartime. The president is the commander in chief, and Congress writes statutes to try to give the president discretion to make the policies that will help win the war on terrorism."

"BUSH TO UN: DROP DEAD"*

The American claim to moral superiority, battered by Rwanda but still relatively strong by the end of the Clinton era, lies in tatters at

---

*This memorable headline is from a *Slate* feature on John Bolton, published March 7, 2005.

the end of 2005. With it in the international gutter lies the popularity of Americans (in general) and our government, specifically.

On one hand, the modern pro-Bush conservative is right to point to plunging popularity polls and scoff. American foreign policy isn't *American Idol;* Gambia, France, and Nepal aren't going to call in, vote for our performance, and make us all winners.

On the other hand, the modern conservative is wrong to sneer at those plunging numbers without thinking about the political trends that have driven them down—and where those dissatisfied foreigners might start putting their time and money if America is viewed as old and busted.

The world views the invasion of Iraq as a war of exploitation sold with lies. All future U.S. military interventions will be seen as potentially "more of the same," and it will be far harder for allies to rally to our cause when their own voters view that cause as corrupt.

The world views the United States as having declared a virtual war on the UN, evading its dues, nominating John "Don't make me angry, you wouldn't like me when I'm angry" Bolton as its UN ambassador.

Bolton's appointment to the UN is a message in itself. As *Slate* reminded us in March 2005, Bolton said publicly that "there is no such thing as the United Nations. . . . If the UN Secretariat Building in New York lost ten stories, it wouldn't make a bit of difference." Worse, he believed that "it is a big mistake for us to grant any validity to international law even when it may seem in our short-term interest to do so—because, over the long term, the goal of those who think that international law really means anything are those who want to constrain the United States."

Actually, the last thing the Founding Fathers wanted to see was the United States as global colossus, embroiled in low-intensity conflicts around the world while trying to maintain a stable of allies and client states, one that viewed international law with contempt. They were familiar with a power of that nature during their own time period. It was called the British Empire. There was much to admire about the empire's methods of political and economic management, but much to loathe about the human rights violations, wars, and exploitation that it left in its wake, so the Framers hoped to appropriate the former without also adopting the latter.

But let's revisit the reasons why the Founders felt recognition of international law and treaty to be a vital element in a healthy country: without that recognition, effective diplomacy is impossible, and war far more likely.

As a result of the Bush administration's decision to plow forward on its own course, despite the legitimate misgivings of the international community, the world sees images of American troops bombing Afghan villages and shooting Iraqis. Now America isn't an outside power that can bring peace to the Middle East by leading negotiations between the Palestinians and the Israelis—it's part of Team Alpha (Israel + U.S.! Go, Team Alpha!), a Western/Jewish conspiracy against Team Beta (all the angry Muslim fundamentalists across the Middle East, Central Asia, and Southeast Asia).

The world sees images of tortured prisoners at Abu Ghraib and hears about the rights systematically stripped from detainees at Guantánamo Bay. America can no longer tell an autocrat in a country such as Zimbabwe or Burma that he's violating his own people's human rights without them loudly rallying their own people against the "hypocrisy" of a corrupt country that only protects human rights when it's convenient.

Suddenly, countries such as Canada, Australia, New Zealand,

and the Scandinavian bloc are looking pretty attractive to entrepreneurs, artists, and students who seek a better life somewhere with a strong economy and good human rights. And increasingly, instead of attending American universities and learning about the Western world at Yale, or at Georgetown, or at the University of Michigan–Ann Arbor, foreign students are staying in their home countries and listening to lectures about the need for a new global counterbalance to American power gone wild.

You can disregard world opinion for a year, no sweat. For an entire presidential term, sure. For a decade? By 2010, we may be collectively in for some rough sailing, especially with our ship—once strong and built with the strongest materials hewn from the ideas of the Enlightenment—leaking.

Of course, when we're talking about business, money, oil, and other more important matters, right-wingers proclaim Bush and Company doing the Founders' work. Take an article that appeared in *National Review* in 2005, written by a professor of international trade law at Northwestern University.

"As Congress begins to debate CAFTA, President Bush's trade policy should be celebrated for what it is—a bold return to the outlook on trade embraced by our Founding Fathers," John McGinnis wrote. "President Bush's policy most resembles the outlook of one previous American government: the Continental Congress of 1776. And President Bush's reasons for liberalizing trade with many nations are very similar to those offered by such luminaries as Ben Franklin, John Adams, and Thomas Jefferson in the early days of the republic."

What McGinnis is talking about is the "Model Treaty," a piece of legislation the new Congress passed, which promoted liberal "trade treaties" between the United States and countries around the world. However, what McGinnis doesn't mention is that that same Congress also respected other types of treaties (in later years, they violated treaties made with American Indians, of course)—those having little to do with money and everything to do with keeping the peace.

2001 Energy Task Force: A Thriller

WRITER: I have a great idea for a new political thriller.

PRODUCER: I'm listening.

WRITER: It's called *The Task Force*.

PRODUCER: Okay, this could be good. Let me guess: A rogue military unit of misfit-but-elite soldiers, breaking all the rules, has to race against time and its own well-meaning but bumbling government to stop a nuclear bomb from being detonated in New York City.

WRITER: Well, not exactly. Try this on for size: The vice president of the United States is a former CEO of a major corporation with deep ties to the energy industry. In his first few months in office, he gathers a task force of government officials and industry executives to set the energy policy of the United States. The meetings are completely secret, and no environmentalists or members of the media have access.

Flash forward: The existence of the task force slips out, and there's a Supreme Court lawsuit to open the records. The vice president goes duck hunting with one of the justices, and fixes things so the suit fails.

Flash forward again: A courageous Democratic candidate, campaigning on the people's right to know their own government, and hearkening back to the values of America's Founding Fathers, wins the election and opens the records. Corruption is exposed; the vice president has a heart attack and falls out of a helicopter.

PRODUCER: [laughs condescendingly] Interesting but plausible. The Democratic candidate character is completely unrealistic. How about superspy Jack Ryan?

WRITER: All right, we'll go with superspy Jack Ryan.

PRODUCER: Great. And we'll probably do a little bit of rewriting so that the plot is a little bit more angled toward the nuclear-weapon thing, and a little bit less angled toward the energy-task-force thing.

WRITER: Sounds good. I take cash or checks.

TEN

POOR RICHARD'S ALMANACK AND RICH RICHARD'S ROLODEX

I have no financial interest in Halliburton of any kind and haven't had, now, for over three years.

—Vice President Dick Cheney, September 2003
(His Halliburton stock options soared to $9.2 million in 2005.)

He that is of the opinion money will do everything may well be suspected of doing everything for money.

—Benjamin Franklin

M ONEY—AND HOW YOU MAKE IT—are two of the keys to the American character. This fact was not lost on Dick Cheney and George Bush, who proudly sold themselves to the American public as former CEOs. They could take care of business; they could take care of you. Or: you could take care of yourself while they took care of business, and by taking care of business, you would be able to take care of yourself.

The ties between money and politics are not new. The American Revolution was spurred, in large part, by crushing tariffs and taxes imposed upon the thirteen colonies by their imperial masters in

Britain. The Boston Tea Party was a major act of subversion, and sparked the beginning of the American rebellion against the British. And it all came down to money. Clearly the profit motive dates back to square one.

FRIENDS IN HIGH PLACES

The Founding Fathers were known chiefly for their political idealism and physical courage, not their wealth. But when they entered business, or regulated commerce, they generally acted in ways that benefited the public at large. In the centuries since the Revolution, the opportunity to make money has brought the world's best and brightest to America's doors. Talented immigrants, creative inventors, and incurable workaholics have made the United States an international economic powerhouse, and, indeed, defined the "American dream" of hard work rewarded by iPods, Xboxes, and modestly sprawling McMansions.

On the surface of things, business is business, and a dollar is a dollar. But there are two fundamentally different ways to look at the creation of wealth. The first is to view it as a function of improving society. You can create a good that people want. You can create a process that creates goods or streamlines services in an efficient way. You can make and sell art or literature that people are interested in experiencing. You can increase the speed or reliability of the delivery of goods to remote areas.

In short, you can do something productive for society, and people will pay you for it. This model—the "old-fashioned business ideal"—is the mantle that Cheney and Bush have wrapped themselves in. From this perspective, it's not hard to understand why they might consider consuming goods an act of patriotism.

American ingenuity—not greed—once formed the basis of this business model. And Ben Franklin—with his efforts to establish a postal service, his numerous life-improving inventions, and his brilliantly marketed *Poor Richard's Almanack,* a collection of business and morality tips—is the archetype for this model.

Born in 1706 the tenth son of a Boston candle maker, Franklin had talent aplenty, but lacked the family background that would preordain him for wealth or power. His inventive streak kicked in early; in 1717, at the age of eleven, he invented a pair of swim fins for hands. His younger years included bouts of Deism and vegetarianism, a journalist older brother jailed for protecting a source from the colonial authorities, and exile from a Puritanical Boston that wasn't ready for his offensive brand of free thought.

But he rose from his checkered beginnings to his eventual hallowed spot as the Official Funny Fat Guy of the Founding Fathers and the nation's inspirational folksy old bastard. Combine the inventiveness of Steve Jobs, the calculated folksy charm of Garrison Keillor, the countercultural chops of Kurt Vonnegut, and the media savvy of Bono, and you begin to get a sense of Benjamin Franklin's style and impact. In his latter days, at the height of his popularity, he drew crowds by merely stepping outside to take a walk.

The consummate man of pragmatic industry among a very industrious and pragmatic bunch of folks, Franklin was the first face that independent America fully presented to the world. When the American frontier philosopher met up with Voltaire in Paris in 1778, it resonated in the popular imagination. The pioneer philosopher who faced down the British Empire had finally come face-to-face with the jocular tormentor of priests and kings.

He wrote to his daughter about the attention he received while in France: "My picture is everywhere, on the lids of snuff boxes, on rings, busts. The numbers sold are incredible. My portrait is a best seller, you have prints, and copies of prints and copies of copies spread everywhere. Your father's face is now as well known as the man in the moon." (Contrast this with the modern era, of course, where an American leader traveling abroad is more likely to touch off a three-day riot than a rush for commemorative souvenirs.)

Part of the excitement about Franklin stemmed from his connection to the new continent's obvious commercial and scientific potential. From its bursting natural resources to its endless tracts of fertile land to its mineral resources to its hearty colonists, it was clear that America was a smart bet for the future.

That bet was placed, in part, on the American spirit of innovation that Franklin, more than any other Founder, came to represent. By now, it's common knowledge that his experimentation with electricity led to his invention of the lightning rod. But fewer know about his invention of a flexible urinary catheter to help his brother, who was beset by kidney stones. Or how he formed the first American fire insurance company. Or how he invented a new kind of carriage odometer that would help calculate routes for delivering mail. These are the kind of commercial innovations that create jobs, distribution systems, and the improvement of society as a whole. In short: beneficial commercial enterprise.

In 1742, Franklin invented an open stove that would efficiently warm rooms in addition to cooking food. To promote the stove (which was becoming popular throughout the colonies), Franklin wrote a pamphlet with the catchy title "An Account of the New-

Invented Pennsylvania Fireplaces: Where Their Construction and Manner of Operation is Particularly Explained, Their Advantages above Every Other Method of Warming Rooms Demonstrated; and All Objections That Have Been Raised against the Use of Them Answered and Obviated, etc." The pamphlet spurred interest in the stove, and a colonial governor offered to give Franklin a patent so that he could be the sole vendor of the stoves for a period of some years and make a considerable fortune.

Franklin declined.

"I declined it from a principle which as ever weighed with me on such occasions," he wrote in his autobiography, "viz. that as we enjoy great advantages from the inventions of others, we should be glad of an opportunity to serve others by any invention of ours, and this we should do freely and generously."

Instead of inventing something new to benefit a single person, and strictly controlling the spread and improvement of technology, why not let it be used and enjoyed by all, improved by anyone with the time and mind power to do so? (Linus Torvalds, the visionary who invented Linux, and thereby goosed the "open source" software movement into global prominence, would later do the same thing.)

It's a philosophy that has helped the world scientific establishment steadily understand more and more about the world we live in, fighting disease and discovering innovations that have been the wellspring for tens of thousands of useful products and processes. Ideas are shared, notes are made generally available, experiments are re-created, and modern scientists stand upon the shoulders of giants who stood upon the shoulders of giants who stood upon the shoulders of Newton, Copernicus, Galileo, Bacon, and Darwin. But in today's business climate, and with the help of "pro-business"

presidents like Bush, we have come to adhere to the Microsoft/
Halliburton/Disney philosophy of business: Make everything pro-
prietary. Sue or compete your opponents into the ground. Change
copyright law so that the copyrights and information existing within
the public domain shrinks and the pockets of private businessmen
swell. Use government contacts to line up no-bid contracts you may
or may not be best qualified to fill. In fact, this has become the dom-
inating economic philosophy in America.

FAVORS, FRIENDS, AND
(OFFSHORE) FORTUNES

Bush's "CEO presidency" has run on the rails of this business policy. You can use political influence to convince the government to
give your already thriving industry subsidies. You can hide money
offshore to avoid taxes, as many of our nation's wealthiest residents
do. You can mark up prices in response to natural disasters (think
Enron), or speculate on inside information (like Bush's magically
fortuitous sale of Harken Oil and Gas stock in 1990 before it
went busto).

In short, you can do something that takes advantage of your existing wealth and political connections, and then make money off
of it. It can't be said that speculation, across the board, is "bad"—
sometimes, well-connected arbitrageurs bring about the confluence
of capital and government deregulation necessary to start a new
sector of the economy ablaze in productive growth.

But not typically.

What the "CEO president" and vice president have done is to
painstakingly build a myth. The myth is that they're "pro-business."

Particularly pro–small business, standing up for the mom-and-pops that hold neighborhoods together and grow up to be innovative new big business.

The record, however, says something different. It tells us that the Bush administration has been overwhelmingly pro-crony, and there's a world of difference between "pro-crony" and "pro-business." A pro-business president levels the playing field by knocking down government subsidies to thriving industries, and by barring special favors that create unfair competition or even monopoly-like situations.

If you're pro-business, in a classic, Founding Father sense, the economic climate improves and everybody wins. If you're pro-crony in a modern corporate/political sense, everyone—except for the president's friends—loses. A perusal of the Bush business record reveals a checkered history that is far from the enlightened capitalist crusade trumpeted in Bush/Cheney campaign materials.

One of President Bush's earliest presidential actions was to demote from his cabinet the head of the Small Business Administration (SBA). This position was boosted to cabinet-level status under President Clinton, a guy who was legitimately good for business and the economy.

In May 2001, *The Washington Post* reported that the administration was seeking to cut the SBA budget by 40 percent. It also planned to cut a $144.5 million appropriation for a small business loan guaranty program and impose higher fees for certain borrowers. Fortunately, both parties in Congress were able to rally around the program and save it. But the effort to kill it in the first place raises some serious questions.

In the wake of Hurricanes Katrina and Rita, Senator John Kerry coauthored an assistance package for small businesses that had been adversely affected. The package—part of a bill funding the Small Business Administration—had previously been approved by the Senate in a 96–0 vote. The Bush administration stripped the package from the final version of the bill.

"The entrepreneurs in the Gulf Coast need contracts, they need business support, and most urgently they need loans," said Kerry. "Yet sixty-seven days after Hurricane Katrina hit the Gulf Coast, the SBA has approved just 593 of the 27,293 loan applications they received—less than 2.5 percent. Unless this aid package is passed into law, it will take years for the SBA to provide this assistance."

Joel Friedman, an analyst for the Center on Budget and Policy Priorities, analyzed Bush's reduction in the top income tax rate and repeal of the estate tax to see if they helped small businesses. Here's what he found:

> *An examination of the relevant data demonstrates that the Administration's statements seriously exaggerate the benefits of its tax cuts—and especially of the top-rate reduction and estate tax repeal—to the vast majority of small businesses.*
>
> *Claims that the top-rate reduction and estate tax repeal are of substantial benefit to small-business enterprises hold true primarily for a small, rather elite group of businesses—those whose owners have very high incomes and have accumulated significant wealth.* For the overwhelming majority of households with small-business income—about 99 percent of them—the reduction in the top income tax rate and the repeal of the estate tax offer no benefits at all [emphasis mine].

On the international scene, the waters for U.S. businesses operating abroad have become polluted by a growing sense of anti-American sentiment. Doing business with America has become an increasingly nauseating act for many countries with Iraq and its attendant scandals all over the headlines. A 2004 survey of eight thousand international consumers released by Seattle-based Global Market Insite noted:

> One-third of all consumers in Canada, China, France, Germany, Japan, Russia, and the United Kingdom said that US foreign policy, particularly the "war on terror" and the occupation of Iraq, constituted their strongest impression of the United States. . . . "Unfortunately, current American foreign policy is viewed by international consumers as a significant negative, when it used to be a positive," comments Dr. Mitchell Eggers, GMI's chief operating officer and chief pollster.

The most dramatic manifestation of this trend is the firebombing of American fast-food restaurants such as KFC and McDonald's, particularly in Muslim countries. And for every Molotov cocktail hurled at a deep fat fryer, ten thousand less excitable consumers turn away from American products and spend their dinars, euros, or rupees elsewhere.

The bigger picture for U.S. business goes beyond the nasty aftertaste of Iraq's occupation. Under President Bill Clinton, America was the world's foremost backer of a comprehensive international rules-based system of free trade. Whether you love globalization or hate it, you have to acknowledge the myriad advantages it offered U.S. companies doing business abroad, including legal protections, easily facilitated multinational deals, and a framework for mediation.

The Bush administration's "my way or the highway" model, by contrast, has led to incidents such as Canada increasing its oil exports to China in protest of America's refusal to let Canadian timber companies compete (and yes, sometimes beat) American companies by producing a better commodity at a lower price. Protectionism has its benefits, but generations of economists have recognized that its costs are inevitably greater.

PROFITEERING PUBLIC SERVANTS

On September 15, 2005, Senator Frank Lautenberg congratulated Vice President Cheney for making money the new-fashioned way—speculating on contracts thrown by the government to his old employer. The value of Cheney's Halliburton stock options has exploded in the wake of lucrative contracts given out by the very government Cheney is co-helming. At the time of Lautenberg's statement, the vice president continued to hold 433,333 Halliburton stock options, worth $9,214,154.93.

"Halliburton has already raked in more than $10 billion from the Bush–Cheney administration for work in Iraq, and now they are being awarded some of the first Katrina contracts," said Lautenberg. "It is unseemly for the vice president to continue to benefit from this company at the same time his administration funnels billions of dollars to it."

It may be indelicate to suggest impropriety simply because the vice president takes hundreds of thousands of dollars in stock gains and deferred salary payments from a company doing lucrative business with the government during times of crisis, but . . . hell. Someone should probably mention it. It's juicy stuff.

James Surowiecki, writing in a "Talk of the Town" piece in the September 2, 2002 issue of *The New Yorker,* put his finger on the problems that have slipped into the halls of government on the heels of Bush's "big business" team:

> *Almost none of the C.E.O.s on the Bush team headed competitive, entrepreneurial businesses. The majority of them, in fact, made their bones in protected or regulated industries, where success depends on personal lobbying and political maneuvering. . . . David Lesar [Cheney's successor at Halliburton] has said, "What Dick brought was obviously a wealth of contacts." Wealth of contacts, indeed: under Cheney, Halliburton expanded internationally, gained $1.5 billion in subsidies from the U.S. government, and added a billion dollars in government contracts.*

This doesn't mean that Cheney's tenure at Halliburton was an unmitigated success. His big accomplishment was the $7.7 billion acquisition in 1998 of Dresser Industries. That hot new property turned out to be loaded down with asbestos-related liabilities.

Naturally, Dick Cheney and Halliburton, before his departure to help run the country, contributed more than $150,000 to members of Congress who sponsored legislation that would limit the ability of workers to sue companies for asbestos exposure. After all, if the choice is between protecting the physical health of workers, and protecting the financial health of a corporation, isn't the decision pretty clear?

THE OIL TYKE-OON

The CEO vice president has been often (and rightfully) dragged through the coals for the conflict between his private business and the public good. But what of the president himself?

His own spectacularly unsuccessful forays into the oil business have been well documented, but what really matters in terms of his public service are the "CEO" attributes he's carried into the White House. In *The Price of Loyalty*—Ron Suskind's account of Paul O'Neill's time as treasury secretary—Bush's "CEO as autocrat" model is lined up against O'Neill's "CEO as informed leader" ideal.

In Bush's mind, being a CEO leader means dressing neatly, showing up for meetings on time, and never diverging from the agenda. It means setting the agenda from the top down, subordinates who never contradict the boss, and sweeping arguments under the rug. It means doing and dying by personal loyalty: no matter what your sins or weaknesses, you'll be Taken Care Of if you're good and you go along with the program, and no matter how smart or talented you are, you'll be "taken care of" if you openly challenge the leader. Speaking up, even in private, is a vice.

The ultimate example of this was the demotion of Bunnatine ("Bunny") Greenhouse. As the top official at the U.S. Army Corps of Engineers, she was in charge of awarding government contracts for the reconstruction of Iraq. She'd served her country for twenty years, and probably felt like she knew her way around government contracts—a view her stellar job evaluations seemed to support. That proved to be her undoing. She made a critical mistake: she objected to secret, no-bid contracts awarded to Kellogg Brown & Root (KBR), a subsidiary of Halliburton. There was no room for this sort of opposition in an administration that put loyalty to private profits before loyalty to the public good. In August 2005, she was bumped from her position to a lesser post in the civil works division of the corps.

This wouldn't have been the case in a Paul O'Neill administration. CEO O'Neill—like George Washington—grappled openly with problems, getting as much hard data as possible, and having bright minds fight out the pros and cons of different solutions. That means stocking your board with challenging subordinates who aren't afraid to deliver bad news and admit that sometimes reality gets the better of even the most exciting and inspirational of ideological plans. Speaking up is a virtue. It helps determine the truth.

Under O'Neill's thirteen-year stewardship of the aluminum giant Alcoa, the company made a historic turnaround. It went from $1.1 million in earnings in 1987 to $1.5 billion in 2000. In that year Alcoa was the best performing stock on the NYSE.

Under Bush and Cheney's stewardship, the national budget has exploded, a war was fought on the basis of bad, largely uncorroborated intelligence, and a hurricane that was necessarily going to be bad was made far more hideous by both pre and post facto mismanagement from the top.

Naturally, O'Neill was quickly drummed out of office after twenty-three months in government for not marching to the beat.

Although America's founders are remembered today mostly for their devotion to individual liberties and their military fight against the British Empire, their contributions to the country's long-term economic health can't be overlooked.

You want American business savvy? Franklin had American business savvy. He understood innovation. He understood the shared wealth of the public domain. He understood how to scratch together a living using his wits.

Alexander Hamilton, architect of our modern banking and securities institutions, had it, too. He understood credit and debt. He understood smart regulation, and smart revenue management. He understood the tricky gray areas between starvation, taxation, and annexation, and how to keep the federal government strong without making private industry weak.

The people who lack this knowledge and understanding on the modern scene are—ironically—exactly the same dudes who are trumpeting their knowledge and understanding the loudest, while spending most of their free energy fighting on behalf of specific donors, not struggling industries or small businesses, who need the most help.

America's founders acknowledged the critical importance of keeping public service and private profit at arm's length—or farther—from each other. In a draft of his farewell address, Washington noted:

"If my country has derived no benefit from my services, my fortune, in a pecuniary point of view, has received no augmentation from my country."

Can Dick Cheney say the same thing with a straight face?

THE 𝔄lternate 𝔘niverse DAILY SPECTATOR

DECEMBER 20, 2004

Bush Social Security Plan:
Steady As She Goes

WASHINGTON, D.C.—Bucking backers who have called for the privatization of Social Security, President Bush announced today that he was proposing no major changes to the popular government program.

"I've looked at the numbers," said the president, "and they aren't too bad. According to the Congressional Budget Office, the system will still be paying full benefits until the year 2052, at which point they'd drop to about 78 percent of the promised amount. But benefits will have been increasing steadily up until then, so the cut will be negligible."

The president cited a recent biography of Alexander Hamilton written by Ron Chernow as part of his inspiration to leave the program intact. "Hamilton, he—he really dug into the numbers before making an economic decision. He read like crazy. I did, too, as best I could—I'm not Hamilton, but I talked to a lot of smart people who understand economics, and they kept saying: 'Medicare, that's your problem. Health care is in trouble. Americans need affordable health care. Social Security, that can wait.'"

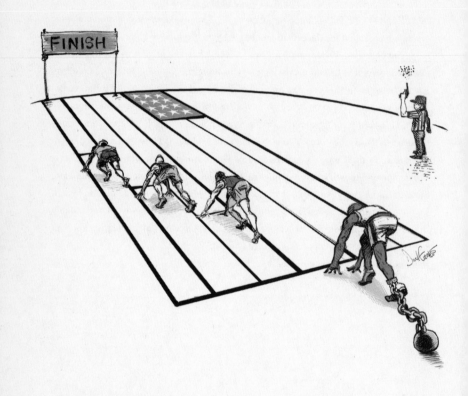

ELEVEN

SLAVES, SUBJECTS, AND CITIZENS

All hereditary Government is in its nature tyranny.... To inherit a Government, is to inherit the people, as if they were flocks and herds.

—Tom Paine, *Rights of Man*

After all, [Saddam Hussein] is the guy who tried to kill my dad.

—George W. Bush, September 26, 2002

WHETHER YOU'RE WOLFING DOWN borscht in Moscow under the rule of Ivan the Terrible surrounded by people for whom political equality is an optimistic fiction or sipping a latte in downtown Seattle surrounded by people for whom a broken espresso machine is a morale-crushing tragedy, every citizen's (or subject's) impact on their government varies. Political power varies with wealth, with the changing of a last name, and with the rise and fall of personal political connections and activism. A czar and a serf sat at opposite ends of a long spectrum of political influence during the era of monarchal Russia; a billionaire baron of information technology and a mentally ill homeless person sit at opposite ends in Seattle.

What about the spectrum of power that falls between those two extremes, between the titans and the helpless? How generously is real power spread around? Who has the ability to speak out and be heard? Whose vote is important and whose is purged from the voter rolls? Who is entitled to know just what the hell is going on with his government?

Throughout history, there have been three basic categories of great political reapportionments of power. Revolutions are the first, the kinds of uprisings that have ripped the concentrated power out of the hands of monarchs or despots and put it into the hands of the public, greatly increasing the amount of equality and representation (such as the American Revolution and the fall of Communism in Eastern Europe). Some revolutions have just shifted the power from one elite to another, such as the Russian Revolution, which took absolute power from the czar and his advisers, and moved it to Lenin and the Politburo. And then there are the revolutions that have taken power away from the many and delivered it to the few, as in Caesar's rise to become dictator of Rome, and the ascent of Mussolini in Italy and of Augusto Pinochet in Chile.

Under the Bush administration, many of the indicators of a free society—government accountability, the right to speak and assemble freely, fair and speedy trials, the equitable distribution of public money for the public good, governmental checks and balances—have been waning.

If freedom is a mixing board, the Founding Fathers pushed almost every slider toward "liberty." The last five years of government have seen almost every slider pushed in the opposite direction, and that should be of concern to all Americans—Democrats, libertarians, independents, moderate Republicans, and even doctrinaire, old-school conservatives.

Let's take a look at some relevant issues: government transparency, free press, the treatment of prisoners of war, and the overall flow of political power and access, and how the ideals of the Founders are being betrayed. But before we can compare apples to apples, there's an ugly sack of oranges that needs to be talked about.

SLAVERY

For all their florid rhetoric—and the amount of good that their pragmatism, basic decency, and brilliant government planning managed to accomplish—it's a mistake to celebrate the Founding Fathers uncritically. Although they didn't institute the cruel practice of human slavery (we have the British to thank for that early American tragedy), they also didn't apply the brakes. A provision in the Constitution that stopped Congress from banning the importation of slaves until 1808 was a critical compromise from the perspective of Southern states, and a rare abridgement of Congress's right to legislate freely. Worse, the 1808 importation ban didn't halt the domestic slave trade, or even American involvement in slave trading overseas.

The Constitution also contained the infamous "federal ratio," which assigned slaves a value of three-fifths of a human being. This assignation was determined in terms of political representation (via plantation owners) and taxation. The Three-Fifths Compromise is a bleak moment in the history of early America. A careful examination of the personal writings of many of the Founders will yield clear, and often passionate, opposition views to slavery from

Benjamin Franklin, Thomas Paine, John Jay, and Alexander Hamilton. On the other end of the spectrum, you'll find verbal flourishes in defense of individual rights belied by personal ownership of slave-worked plantations—Thomas Jefferson and James Madison stand among the worst offenders on this count. Jefferson's vicious description of blacks in *Notes on the State of Virginia* will evoke a shudder of disgust from even his biggest fans.

> *Never yet could I find a black had uttered a thought above the level of plain narration; never see even an elementary trait of painting or sculpture. . . . Misery is often the parent of the most affecting touches in poetry—Among the blacks is misery enough, God knows, but no poetry. Their love is ardent, but it kindles the senses only, not the imagination.*

And this is just the one nut in the fruitcake. Madison, for his part, spoke often against slavery as an evil. But during the Missouri Crisis of 1819–1821 (when debate raged as to whether it should be admitted as a free or slave state), Madison denied that Congress could attach an antislavery condition to the admission of a new state, or control the migration of slaves within the several states. He questioned the constitutionality of laws excluding slavery from the national territories, and even suggested that the expansion and dispersion of slavery would improve the condition of the slaves and hasten the end of the institution of slavery itself.[61]

> *. . . I have certainly felt all the influence that cd justly flow from a conviction, that an uncontrouled dispersion of the slaves now in the US was not only best for the nation, but most favorable to the slaves, also both as to their*

*prospects for emancipation, and as to their condition in the
mean time.*

In his will, Madison (unlike Washington) refused to emancipate
his slaves. He would look out for their best interest by ensuring
they would have a happy home under the thumb of his wife, their
new owner.

Of course it's easy to look back at individuals from a different
time, where institutions and individuals operated in a thoroughly
different context, and condemn them by holding them to modern
standards. You want them to have been so ahead of their time, so
enlightened that they were capable of seeing beyond their societal
context. But many of them weren't.

Madison and Jefferson had complicated, checkered, and sometimes disgraceful personal and political records on the issue.* In
fact, collectively, the Founding Fathers have to answer for incor-
porating the United States while slavery was still an accepted and
legal institution.

But if you consider the debates raging during that hot
Philadelphia summer of 1776 at the Constitutional Convention,
and consider along with it the political forces in play, you realize
that simply uniting thirteen colonies under a federal government,
with or without slavery, was a miraculous achievement. It was a
compromise made possible only by the lingering camaraderie of
the Revolutionary War, of the tactical and strategic political, if not
moral, brilliance of Madison and Hamilton, and of the trust that
nearly all prominent Americans had in George Washington.

---

*Some others of the Founders, such as Washington and Paine, however, held true to their con-
demnatory words for the institution of slavery. Benjamin Franklin was a fierce moral opponent of slavery.

Seen in this light, absent the egregious error of ratifying the Constitution with slavery still a legal practice, the ratification itself was a massive political victory for liberty, won by the scantest of margins.

INDIANS AND IRAQIS

American historians typically—and correctly—classify the dealings of European colonists with the Native Americans into the category of Things We Should Be Ashamed Of. There's no question that the bulk of the white man's contact with their Native American brethren has been distinguished by massive fraud, brutal violence, a desire for eradication, and finally, outright cultural imperialism. At the same time, those who depict Native Americans as a saintly population would be making a mistake. Indian tribes made war with one another, often brutalized one another, formed alliances of convenience with European powers, could often be bought and sold for trade goods or political concessions, and so on.

If you were to compare the Founders' stance on Native Americans with the Bush administration's handling of the Sunni population in Iraq, you would find that both the Native Americans and the Sunnis hung around the ragged edge of American military power. That is to say, members of both groups sometimes fought and killed Americans, civilians, and troops alike, and both groups posed a host of political challenges to what can be classified in both cases as an American occupying force.

Despite our federal government's shameful history with America's native peoples, the Founders themselves were gravely concerned with the welfare of the American Indian. In his 1790 Second Annual Message to Congress, George Washington spoke about so-called hostile Indian tribes, whose military attacks had cost numerous American lives. While he called for the mobilization of a militia to defend the frontier, he also recognized that it was critical for the United States to "respect [Indian] rights and reward their attachments."[62]

In a letter written July 20, 1791, Washington blamed much of the frontier trouble on white settlers, who openly despised Native Americans, and their way of living.

> *I must confess I cannot see much prospect of living in tranquility with them so long as a spirt of land jobbing [speculation] prevails, and our frontier Settlers entertain the opinion that there is not the same crime (or indeed no crime at all) in killing an Indian as in killing a white man.*[63]

While later U.S. presidents—notably Andrew Jackson—pursued a policy of eradication (the 1830 Indian Removal Act, for example, which Jackson considered a humanitarian act), the Founders advocated a more enlightened approach. In his Third Annual Message to Congress on October 25, 1791, Washington said that violating the rights of Native Americans (specifically by infringing upon treaties) endangered the peace of the Union. He also lamented the fact that Native Americans lacked an active press, writing:

> *They, poor wretches, have no Press thro' which their grievances are related; and it is well known, that when one side*

*only of a Story is heard, and often repeated, the human
mind becomes impressed with it, insensibly.*

Jefferson, for his part, was a keen student of Native American
languages, culture, and artifacts. He also expressed relief in 1801
that the Native American population was recovering in numbers—
an unfortunate misconception, but one that was cheering rather
than depressing to him. But, in keeping with his complicated rela-
tionships to oppressed groups, Jefferson also wrote, in 1791, that he
hoped U.S. forces would give hostile tribes a "thorough drubbing."
But he then expressed his wish that they then "change our toma-
hawk into a golden chain of friendship."[64]

Although Native Americans posed a real military and political threat to a country dead set on expanding across the continent, the Founders, as individuals and in their policies, did not
dehumanize or target them for eradication. These horrific policies
would, of course, be instituted by later generations of American
leaders.

The mere act of taking up arms against the United States
was not enough to get the entire native population labeled as a
bunch of "dead-enders" with no rights. In many ways, the
Founding Fathers understood the motivation of hostile tribes,
populations whose land had been encroached upon, who were
encountering armed invaders, and who were threatening to
change their lives as they knew it. The Founders earnestly hoped
to find some kind of deeper understanding—and a real peace—
down the road.

This kind of desire for understanding has been elusive in the
Bush administration's handling of some segments of the Iraqi
population.

PRISONERS OF WAR

The way a military treats its prisoners of war is an indication of the fundamental character of that country. By definition, a prisoner of war is not a criminal—instead, he or she is someone captured while fighting on behalf of their society or government. During the American Revolution, British troops treated the captured officers from General Washington's companies with astounding cruelty.

Washington wrote to British commander Thomas Gage on August 11, 1775, complaining of the treatment that captured colonial fighters were receiving.

> *Sir*
>
> *I understand that the Officers engaged in the Cause of Liberty, and their Country, who by the Fortune of War, have fallen into your Hands have been thrown indiscriminately, into a common Gaol appropriated for Felons—That no Consideration has been had for those of the most respectable Rank, when languishing with Wounds and Sickness. That some have even been amputated, in this unworthy Situation.*

Washington threatened to treat British prisoners in similar fashion, yet in a letter sent to Gage eight days later, again pleading for decent treatment of American troops, he all but conceded that the threat was an empty one. He couldn't bring himself to do it.

> *Not only your Officers, and Soldiers have been treated with a Tenderness due to Fellow Citizens, & Brethren; but even*

those execrable Parricides, whose Counsels & Aid have del-
uged their Country with Blood, have been protected from
the Fury of a justly enraged People.[65]

Again and again, Washington emerges as a figure motivated by strict duty toward those who break the rules of war (ordering the execution of deserters and cowards, hanging the dashing and sympathetic British spy Major John André), and a real tenderness toward war's vulnerable victims—most notably prisoners and civilians. Washington understood that the Revolution's success was dependent upon it retaining the moral high ground. (A lesson largely abandoned in the "War on Terror.")

Jefferson, for his part, suggested the Roman practice of torturing slaves to gain evidence was obsolete and morally incorrect, and that it was better not to even use testimony garnered in this fashion. Believe it or not, slaves in Revolutionary times had at least nominally more rights than detainees in Guantánamo Bay or the poor suckers unlucky enough to get dragnetted into Abu Ghraib during the Great Big American Clusterfuck era of its operation.

Those responsible for the abuses in the American military penal system lacked Washington's perspective. Chasing the short-term goal of military information, high-level thinkers such as Alberto Gonzales and Donald Rumsfeld loosened key restrictions that prevented the torture of detainees, thereby doing grave damage to the long-term goal of maintaining America's international prestige and respect. And they set the stage for midlevel players in the military and intelligence services to cast wide nets with low standards, sweeping mostly innocent prisoners into Abu Ghraib and other desolate overseas prisons.

Many older members of Congress, often veterans themselves, raised—and continue to raise—objections to the treatment of captives and detainees. Republican senators John McCain, John Warner, and Lindsey Graham all stood up to the White House on this issue, and showed—in defiance of their own party's leadership—that they understood what was at stake, globally and domestically, in allowing such tactics to continue. The debate, McCain said, "is not about who they are. It's about who we are."[66]

THE TYRANNY OF THE ELITE

"Running against Washington," a political strategy popularized by Jimmy Carter and perfected by Ronald Reagan, has been around since the late eighteenth century. Patrick Henry raged against the Constitution as "the tyranny of Philadelphia," and compared its precepts to "the tyranny of King George III."[67]

Like today's anti–big government Republicans (who, in reality, want a big government that pumps its money into the pockets of right-leaning industrialists and military contractors rather than into social programs or national infrastructure), Henry and other Constitution opponents posed as populists fighting for the "little guy"—while enjoying the backing of major slaveholders; Henry warned slaveholding delegates who supported the ratification of the Constitution that "they'll free your niggers."

But George Washington considered the opposition to the Constitution by slaveholding landholders on populist grounds to be unusual.

"It is a little strange," he wrote to the Marquis de Lafayette in

1788, "that the men of large property in the South should be more afraid that Constitution will produce an aristocracy or a monarchy than the genuine, democratical people of the East."[68]

You may recall a similar situation cropping up in the 2000 and 2004 presidential elections: the political vanguard of the far right—mostly extremely wealthy and well-connected—running "against Washington" and "the elitists."

Since Bush's election to office, however, the number of registered lobbyists in Washington has more than doubled, and the proportion of GOP lobbyists has skyrocketed as Democrats have been systematically elbowed out of the feeding trough.

It's no secret that the confluence of big money, industry, the energy lobby, and the personal Bush political dynasty is currently calling the shots in D.C. In *Federalist No. 62*, James Madison could be tallying the booming post-9/11 fortunes of Halliburton, the oil industry, and the richest tenth of a percent of taxpayers. He wrote:

> *Another effect of public instability is the unreasonable advantage it gives to the sagacious, the enterprising, and the moneyed few over the industrious and uninformed mass of the people. . . .*
>
> *This is a state of things in which it may be said with some truth that laws are made for the few, not for the many.*

THE Alternate Universe DAILY SPECTATOR

OCTOBER 3, 2005

Bush Nominates Respected Moderate for Court Seat

WASHINGTON, D.C.—In a move that puts a well-respected Hispanic jurist on a fast track to the highest judicial office in the land, President Bush today nominated Sonia Sotomayor, a respected jurist of moderate proclivities, to the Supreme Court. Democrats and some moderate Republicans, expecting a hard-line loyalist, greeted the decision with qualified enthusiasm.

Strict judicial originalists have taken issue in the past with Sotomayor's assertion that the law can and should "evolve" as a result of judicial decisions. At today's press conference, Bush rebutted that criticism directly:

"Even the Founding Fathers didn't know what a 'strict interpretation' of the Constitution really meant. Just look at Hamilton and Madison arguing about their own Constitutional intentions just a few years after the document's ratification. Or listen to George Washington talking about its flexibility:

"'Is there not a constitutional door open for alterations or amendments? And is it not likely that real defects will be as readily discovered after as before trial; and will not our successors be as ready to apply the remedy as ourselves if occasion should require it?' Doesn't sound too strict to me, but hey, I'm just a Yale and Harvard grad who got himself elected to the highest office in the land."

Conservatives are threatening to fight Sotomayor's nomination, but some right-leaning commentators have grudgingly admitted her qualifications for the bench.

"She's smart, she's honest, and she has a track record for evenhandedness," said pundit George Will. "But we can't count on her loyalty to modern conservative principles. There's a real danger that she'll follow an interpretation of the law as based on facts, precedent, and the general welfare of Americans, not current right-wing ideology."

TWELVE

THE FOUNDATIONS
OF A COMEBACK

*Some in my party threaten to send a message that they
don't know a just war when they see it, and more broadly
that they're not prepared to use our military strength to
protect our security and the cause of freedom.*
—Senator Joseph Lieberman, July 28, 2003

There was never a good war or a bad peace.
—Benjamin Franklin, September 11, 1783

I T's ALWAYS BEEN a two-man game. The revolutionaries battled
the British. The Federalists bickered with the anti-Federalists.
Jefferson and Hamilton went at it, before Jefferson turned his sights
on Adams. Whigs got into the game. Democrats. Republicans. Et
cetera. Sure, third parties sometimes got past the velvet rope, but
their glory was always short-lived, their access transitory.

There are many in this country who believe giving more people
access to government means opening up the political game to third,
fourth, and fifth parties, and this isn't a bad idea. But right now, we
are watching even the measly two-party system we've operated

within erode and disappear into a crevasse dug by the Republican Party, while the Democrats stand by with their mouths agape, drooling.

In fact, despite all of the rhetoric about a bitter partisan split between Democrats and Republicans, there has, since September 11, 2001, really been only one functional political party in the United States: the Republican Party.

In the years following the invasion of Afghanistan, Republicans have become embroiled in numerous scandals, gone half-mad with paranoia, and stormed across the world to start a war that has provided legions of terrorists with a perfect military training ground and two generations' worth of propaganda material. All in the name of freedom and liberty.

In uncertain times, it's easy to cling to the image of reassuring solidity that Republicans radiate, even during the worst of self-created disaster. Staying the course is infinitely easier than reexamining policy and perhaps making changes.

In the meantime, where have the Democrats been? With pennies from heaven like Tom DeLay's and Scooter Libby's indictments, with Michael Brown and Harriet Miers, with the fog of impropriety surrounding Bill Frist and Dick Cheney, Democrats have chosen to sit quietly in the corner, rocking and mumbling about how Kerry should've been a shoo-in.

During its exile from power, the Democratic Party has been a political party in name only. It's a group in which quasi-conservatives such as Joe Lieberman and Hillary Clinton contribute to Republican disasters, including the invasion of Iraq, while doctrinaire liberals such as Ted Kennedy and Jon Corzine take lonely stands articulating the party's core ideas.

And at a time when the president can still offer a (bad) plan for

Social Security and a (flawed, crippled, but, one hopes, sufficient) plan to move Iraq toward its new life as a stable democratic state, the Democrats are invisible on the national scene as a united force with ideas of their own.

For all their claims to the contrary, today's Republicans are not the "traditionalist" party in the United States. The Democratic Party is. Progressivism isn't a foreign aberration—it is the logical extension of the progressive values of America's founders. In fact, the true Democratic Party is the party of Washington, Hamilton, Franklin, Jefferson, and Paine. It takes as its core values enlightened pragmatism, the protection of personal rights, the honorable and decent treatment of all people—foreign or not, prisoner or free. It aspires to the ascension of the rule of law and expertise over personal loyalty and faction. It's the party of the free press and of transparent government accountable to all of the people—not just its political backers.

In its pure form, it can help American business grow by ensuring a level playing field, while preventing abusive excesses that will, over time, erode the economy, the standards by which workers are treated, and which will lead to an unproductive backlash against industry.

Finally, if it stays true to the vision of America's Founders, the Democratic Party is the political party that understands best the value of vigorous political debate both between and within partisan groups in search of sound policies built on fact, not mere ideology.

PROGRESSIVE THIS

Despite the epithets and insults hurled at Your Average Progressive, chances are he shares more values with the Founders than your dyed-in-the-wool conservative (you know, those guys who insist that they are bringing "dignity back to the White House"). The original progressive values, as envisioned and articulated by the Founders, included individual rights, liberty, dedication to the public good, openness in government, free inquiry, equality of opportunity, and, above all, truth, for truth made the realization of all the aforementioned values possible.

It's interesting, actually, to observe how the right wing, and the Bush administration in particular, have turned Founder values into political liabilities for any politician who dares espouse such values publicly: empathy and understanding, which Washington cultivated among his generals in the midst of a vicious revolutionary war, are seen as tools of the weak-willed and cowardly; promoting equal opportunity, a core value that was undeniably important to the Founders, is deemed "rainbow politics"; demanding transparency in government during a time of war is downright unpatriotic.

These are not obscure, newfangled values. They are not ideological Frankensteins of New Deal idealism and Clintonian compassion. These values are as old as the country itself. They are the ideals of the Founders.

In a speech given at the 2003 Take Back America Conference, Bill Moyers outlined the progressive family tree. Progressives, he said, exalted and extended the American Revolution, and then articulated and acted upon new terms of partnership between people and their political leaders. They demanded the end of any "unholy alliance between government and wealth."

The Founders, Moyers pointed out, had specifically rejected property qualifications for holding political office because they wanted to eradicate the "veneration of wealth" that had led to such inequality under monarchical rule.

"Conservatives," Moyers said, "hijacked the vocabulary of Jeffersonian liberalism and turned words like 'progress,' 'opportunity,' and 'individualism' into tools for making the plunder of America sound like Divine right."[69]

AN AMERICAN CRISIS

Tom Paine, the Founding Pain-in-the-Ass, is perhaps the Original Progressive. And yet it was Ronald Reagan who most famously invoked Paine's name (during the 1980 Republican National Convention). Funny choice, considering how little Paine has in common with the conservative cause. Paine was downright radical: he fostered the love of democracy in the heart of every American who happened upon his political tracts. He was the type of frothing "liberal" the right wing loves to hate, and for many years, they did, trying to eradicate him from the country's collective memory. But at some point, the right wing wised up, and tried to appropriate Paine. They have, incredibly, met with some measure of success in this endeavor, despite Paine's blatantly progressive values and his obvious radicalism.

Harvey J. Kaye, author of *Thomas Paine and the Promise of America,* examines this appropriation of the country's most radical patriot. For all their invocations of his name and his ideals, conservatives truly cannot claim Paine for themselves.

> *Bolstered by capital, firmly in command of the Republican Party, and politically ascendant for a generation, [conservatives] have initiated and instituted policies and programs that fundamentally contradict Paine's own vision and com-*

mitments. They have subordinated the republic—the res
publica, *the public good—to the marketplace and to private
advantage. They have furthered the interests of corporations and the rich over those of working people, their families, unions, and communities, and they have overseen a
concentration of wealth and power that, recalling the
Gilded Age, has corrupted and debilitated American democratic life and politics. They have carried on culture wars
that have divided the nation and undermined the wall separating church and state. Moreover, they have pursued domestic and foreign policies that have made the nation both
less free and less secure politically, economically, environ-
mentally, and militarily. Even as they have spoken of ad-
vancing freedom and empowering citizens, they have sought
to discharge, or at least constrain, America's democratic impulse and aspiration.*[70]

In *The American Crisis*, Tom Paine laid out a clearly articulated
plan for how to assemble an army of American patriots to fight the
British or deal with future military challenges. He analyzed the
proportion of men able to serve; how to ensure that the men were
equipped with the blankets and shoes necessary for fighting in cold
weather; and how to fund the expedition in a manner that was equitable to all citizens involved in the effort. In addition, Paine presented and analyzed the plan in the context of a struggle for
individual liberty and against tyranny.

Paine crafted his plan according to the tenets of individual liberty and in the context of the revolutionary fight against the British.
And he was serious about implementing these changes. They were

not hazy ideals tossed off during a stump speech. They were deeply held beliefs, free of any personal interests Paine may have harbored, any stock he may have held, any sense of entitlement he may have felt, or any ego-driven desires he may have cultivated in private.

It is this ability to courageously present and champion detailed new ideas on a national level that the Democratic Party must somehow rediscover.

I LOVE LIBERTARIANS

There's a certain ruthlessness to dedicated libertarians that scares the bejeezus out of latte-sucking chumps like myself. Most libertarians won't come out and say that if the poor are starving, they may as well hurry up and do it so as to decrease the surplus population—but some will. Everything gets very Darwinian, very quickly—with the implicit conclusion that the strongest have gotten to the top because they deserve to get there.

Might makes right. When the govenment offers a helping hand, it just encourages the weak to keep breathing our air.

It's no coincidence that most of the libertarians I've met seem to be highly paid technical professionals who will do just fine as long as the slightest scrap of civilization still remains. That, or well-armed Coloradans with the pickup trucks, survival gear, and stoic attitude to survive the implosion of society, and emerge as chiefs of their own head-hunting mutant tribes.

For the rest of us, it makes sense to be wary of a philosophy that draws poetic inspiration from *The Fountainhead,* by Ayn Rand, a book with a key "love" scene that involves a woman's getting raped . . . but totally digging it! *Because it's what she secretly wanted!*

And yet, progressive Americans, libertarians are your friends! Perhaps not normally. But absolutely in the here and now. Strange times make strange bedfellows.

In a functioning United States of America, progressives and libertarians should, on most questions of federal entitlements, business regulation, and the extent of government infrastructure, be battling it out like pit bulls and pythons.

Not only is the debate legitimately interesting—at what point is it more humane and/or efficient to let private enterprise and initiative take over what might have otherwise been a government function?—but it's an argument hallowed by the Founding Fathers, who found themselves split by much the same philosophical dilemma.

Here's Thomas Jefferson carrying a libertarianesque banner: "I am not a friend to a very energetic government. It is always oppressive."

And here's George Washington in a 1787 letter to James Madison, writing an almost Rooseveltian big-government rejoinder: "The Men who oppose a strong & energetic government are, in my opinion, narrow minded politicians, or are under the influence of local views."

Two opposing viewpoints, at loggerheads. For now, and forever, we'll have some people saying that government can be the answer to many of our most pressing problems—and others saying it's the *cause* of those problems.

Personally, I'd say that the former group is more "right." But I'd also freely concede that the latter group can absolutely make a strong logical case for their side, and that you can err in either direction.

Libertarians—libertarians in spirit, National Libertarian Party members, and even the libertarian wing of the GOP—would agree that government should be getting less and less interested in the contents of our bedrooms, our totally legitimate basement greenhouses, and our pocketbooks. Government should be shrinking, be less prone to foreign intervention, and more dedicated to preserving our liberties than hobbling them in the name of "Homeland Security."

Progressives would actually agree with a lot of this, but add that government shouldn't necessarily be shrinking—it should be realigning its priorities so that things such as education, the environment, and post-prison rehabilitation get more money, while corporate welfare, massive military contracts, and tax rebates for the wealthy get less.

Any close observer of the Bush administration would concede that it fulfills neither ideal. It does not believe in a limited, cautious, laissez-faire government—it has created a sometimes hilariously Orwellian "Homeland Security" bureaucracy that appears generally as inept as it is wasteful and labyrinthine. Its major accomplishment, Tom Ridge's "Rainbow of Fear," seemed for a while to arbitrarily increase or decrease the terror threat on the basis of political expediency for the administration. Now it's largely forgotten, due to be embraced as kitsch in 2012 on the first edition of VH1's "Totally Aughts!" celebration of the years 2000–2009.

The administration has expended huge piles of money fighting the very first "luxury war" to smoke a personal nemesis of the Bush family and demonstrate how awesome democracy is by touching off years of sectarian and nationalistic violence. And, very memorably, it has not actually put its money into politically useless but ultimately smart projects such as reinforcing the New Orleans levees against the chance of a catastrophic storm. When it comes to handling the public purse, it's been about as cautious as a raccoon in a sack of marshmallows.

Thus, over the past few years, some of the most cogent criticisms of the current political state haven't come from the progressives who most clearly walk in the footsteps of the Washington/ Hamilton/Adams faction of the Founding Fathers. And they haven't come from the shrill, unreconstructed hard left. They've come from libertarians. Walking in the footsteps of Patrick Henry, Thomas Jefferson, and Tom Paine, they embrace the "negative" view of government—that less is almost always better than more.

While working at *The Al Franken Show,* I found myself repeatedly booking fellows from the libertarian Cato Institute or writers from *Reason* magazine. Simply put: They were saying what more Democrats should have been saying, and with more passion, intellectual firepower, and clarity than almost anyone else on the national scene.

Here's a sampling of Cato scholars writing about federal spending in August and September of 2005:

"Congress Should Make Some Sacrifices, Too," by Stephen Slivinski, September 15, 2005.

"Both Parties Find Trough to Their Liking," by Chris Edwards, August 18, 2005.

"Congress's Latest Christmas Tree Bill," by David Boaz, May 13, 2005.

"Pork: A Microcosm of the Overspending Problem," by Chris Edwards, *Cato Institute Tax and Budget Bulletin* no. 24, August 2005.

And here's Cato's Randy Barnett, using the writing of Alexander Hamilton to put the failed Harriet Miers Supreme Court nomination into perspective. I quote him at length because he provides a perfect example of the kind of practical criticism that libertarians have directed at the Bush administration since its love of pork, corruption, and cronyism has become common knowledge.

During the Clinton impeachment imbroglio, Alexander Hamilton's definition of "impeachable offense" from Federalist No. 65 was plastered from one end of the media to the other. With the nomination of Harriet Miers to the Supreme Court, get ready for another passage from Hamilton to get similar play—this one from Federalist No. 76:

"To what purpose then require the co-operation of the Senate? I answer, that the necessity of their concurrence would have a powerful, though, in general, a silent operation. It would be an excellent check upon a spirit of favoritism in the President, and would tend greatly to prevent the appointment of unfit characters from State prejudice, from family connection, from personal attachment, or from a view to popularity. . . . He would be both ashamed and afraid to bring forward, for the most distinguished or lucrative stations, candidates who had no other merit than

that of coming from the same State to which he particularly belonged, or of being in some way or other personally allied to him, *or of possessing the necessary insignificance and pliancy to render them the obsequious instruments of his pleasure"* [emphasis mine].

As the quote from Hamilton suggests, the core purpose of Senate confirmation of presidential nominees is to screen out the appointment of "cronies," which Merriam-Webster's defines as "a close friend especially of long standing." Cronyism is bad not only because it leads to less qualified judges, but also because we want a judiciary with independence from the executive branch.

Barnett, by going back to the writing and intentions of the Founding Fathers, has put his finger on something absolutely vital to good government in the United States. It is critical that different branches of government have the independence to do their jobs correctly without fear of political censure. A Supreme Court that is in political thrall to one party (or worse, one family) is not going to serve the American people who count upon it to be an impartial source of final legal appeal.

When loyalty and personal connection become paramount (as they have with the Bush administration), the machinery of government moves from being a servant of the American people to a united front against the American people. Prosecutors, journalists, citizen advocates—anyone who might seek some kind of accountability or transparency—are the enemies of a government in which personal ties come first, before the public business.

Libertarians know this better than anyone—they decried far less damaging incidents of cronyism in the Clinton White House, and they'll be decrying cronyism in the White House of whoever takes the presidency in 2008. There is a philosophical consistency to libertarians that makes them true friends of liberty—if, at times, consistent pains in the ass for progressives who think that compassionate, intelligent government is the answer for many pressing national crises.

Libertarians have their eyes on the ball when it comes to our civil liberties, too. Here's *Reason* magazine's Jesse Walker, writing on May 27, 2002, and contextualizing the PATRIOT Act from a libertarian perspective.

So what have our intelligence agencies done since September 11?

On one hand, they asked for, and received, a host of new powers in an anti-terror bill, including the right to engage in secret searches, warrantless Internet surveillance, warrantless access to phone records, and a requirement that retailers report "suspicious" customer transactions to the Treasury.

Civil libertarians warned that powers like these could be abused—and, indeed, had been abused at many times in American history. Nonetheless, the USA Patriot Act passed overwhelmingly, with some legislators voting for it without even reading it. Rep. Ron Paul (R-Texas) told Insight *magazine that he was unable to get his hands on a copy of the bill before it passed. "Maybe a handful of staffers actually read it," he said, "but the bill definitely was not available to members before the vote." . . .*

The atrocities of September 11 were not a surveillance failure. They were an analysis failure. Now that we under-

stand that, can't we reconsider the new incursions into our
privacy that our leaders stampeded blindly into law?

Walker's brief (under six hundred words) rant nails the heart of the problem with post-9/11 reaction—lots of dangerous new powers for an unaccountable government that has proved it can't handle the information it already has.

In our modern times, a libertarian spirit does not have to be in conflict with the goals of the Democratic Party—in fact, the two should pull together in 2006 to restore some sanity to government.

Libertarians want to preserve freedom of speech, freedom of assembly, and transparency of government. So do good Democrats. Libertarians want to rein in wasteful spending. So do smart Democrats. Libertarians want to end the rot of cronyism and lobbying that have turned federal government under Bush into an incompetent, dundering mess. So should honorable Democrats. Libertarians are outraged at the way prisoners of war have been abused and deprived of their rights without trial. Democrats should be, too.

But do *most* Democrats line up with the principled libertarians on the issues that matter? That's another question.

THOSE GODDAMN DEMOCRATS

Of late, the Democrats have flaunted their weaknesses—many of which were exacerbated by the raging success of their last president, Bill Clinton. Clinton's domination of the party created a new addiction to power among party members. It was a revolution so focused on attaining and retaining power that dollars and votes became paramount, at the expense of goals such as bettering living standards for working Americans, protecting the rights of minorities, and aggressively regulating the worst excesses of large corporations. This turn toward a poll-driven, centrist, triangulating strategy worked out just great, right up until the charismatic genius at its head retired to Westchester, New York.

A combination of disgust with Clinton's personal failings and the visionless flaccidity of his successors (probably best personified by the heartbreakingly lackluster former Democratic Senate leader, Tom Daschle) has turned many Americans away from the Democratic Party at a time when its power and influence is desperately necessary to curb the worst excesses of a president and party on the rampage.

Let's assume the Republican propaganda is right, and modern Democrats are indeed opportunistic, unprincipled, adrift, leaderless, and interested only in attaining and using power. Bill Clinton was the poster child for these ills, a perfectly constructed political Antichrist. Yet despite all his flaws, the legacy of his presidency hews close to the vision of the Founders.

During his eight years as president, Bill Clinton:

PUT THE ECONOMY ON FIRM FOOTING: Clinton left office with the longest economic boom in United States history unabated. He also left behind a giant and growing budget surplus.

INTERVENED SUCCESSFULLY IN KOSOVO, ON HUMANITARIAN GROUNDS: His NATO-backed initiative, which came to the very clear benefit of threatened Muslim Kosovars, has come to be seen as a brilliant stroke of multilateral humanitarian intervention—both morally decent and pragmatic from an international PR perspective.

APPOINTED QUALIFIED TECHNOCRATS AND EXPERTS TO CRITICAL GOVERN-MENT POSTS: Clinton viewed his ascension to the presidency as a chance to appoint some of the most qualified and brilliant individuals in America to some of the country's most important positions. Though his administration was often torn by leaks, internal dissent, and disorganization, it also oversaw improvements in pollution standards, a booming economy, the protection of natural resources and species, and fundamental welfare reform.

He also presided over the country at the time of the first Twin Towers bombing in 1993. But despite managing to preside over the capture and conviction of six Islamist extremist conspirators involved in the bombing, he failed to apprehend Osama bin Laden.

However, it is interesting to note that Clinton specifically aligned himself with Thomas Jefferson, explicitly taking him as a presidential role model (a model he followed all too well, in some cases). Many of his policies reflect the kinds of policies Jefferson created or endorsed.

George W. Bush, on the other hand, is, for many Democrats and liberals, another perfectly constructed political Antichrist. His "brain," Karl Rove, takes no Founding Father or Framer as his political and moral compass. Instead, he openly worships Mark Hanna as his political idol. Hanna was a late-nineteenth-century industrialist who oversaw the presidential day-to-days of President McKinley and who was responsible for literally remaking the Republican Party from the party of Lincoln to the party of Reagan and Bush.

During Bush's first five years as president, he and the members of his party:

WILDLY INFLATED THE SIZE OF THE NATIONAL DEBT: It has ballooned to well over $7 trillion as of 2005. When Bush was asked at a press conference, "Who is going to have to pay for this recovery [from Hurricane Katrina]? And what's it going to do to the national debt?" he answered: "It's going to cost whatever it costs." Multiply this approach by Homeland Security, the war in Iraq, the tax cuts for the ultrarich, and you have the root of generations of future economic problems.

INTERVENED CATASTROPHICALLY IN IRAQ: By conflating flawed or fraudulent reports of WMD and insubstantial (and ultimately noncredible) reports of links with Al Qaeda, Bush managed to sell the country on a war that has done much to strengthen Islamic terrorists, and much to destroy the image of the United States overseas— at the cost of hundreds of billions of dollars, thousands of U.S. lives, and tens of thousands of (often innocent) Iráqi lives.

STAFFED EVEN TECHNICAL, NONPARTISAN GOVERNMENT APPOINTEE SLOTS WITH CRONIES: The meteoric rise of Alberto "Torture Memo" Gonzales to the post of attorney general, the mystifying nomination of the lovably clueless Harriet Miers to the Supreme Court, and the appointment of failed horse association president Michael Brown to FEMA are just a few of the most prominent examples of a government run by former industry lobbyists and partisan stooges.

He also presided over the country at the time of the September 11 attacks; and failed to apprehend Osama bin Laden by thoroughly muffing the military endgame at Tora Bora in Afghanistan—a disaster that, unsurprisingly, no one was held accountable for.

Despite this track record, Bush and Company aren't going anywhere. But there may be hope. In his latest book, *The Truth, with Jokes,* Al Franken suggests that belief in a popular Democratic revival may be more than a pipe dream. While voters over thirty went for Bush in 2004 by a seven-point margin, the under-thirty vote went for Kerry by a nine-point margin: 54 percent to 45 percent. Youth turnout boomed in the 2004 election, and Democrats picked up more than sixty seats in state legislatures, particularly out West, where libertarian-leaning independents have become increasingly aware of the threat the modern "conservative" movement poses to truly conservative ideas. And while Al Gore had only gotten contributions from 155,000 people, Kerry took money from well over a million.

The point is, the young people are getting it. And as the conservative movement becomes torn between the huge but dwindling tribe of Bush Republican Party loyalists and intellectual conservatives, more and more people are ready for a change. If the Democrats' new generation of leaders are willing to pick up the standard of the original American Revolution, they could create a second great surge toward equality and reason at the beginning of the twenty-first century.

And why shouldn't that surge happen? Things kind of suck right now. Iraq. Hurricane Katrina. The preference of dogma over science. The exploding federal budget. Critics punished by federal employees for voicing honest concerns. Unqualified losers appointed to vitally important posts. Legislation that rolls back our civil liberties.

But the brilliant system designed by our bewigged forefathers isn't so fragile that these attacks can destroy it.

We still have a free press. Yes, it may be consolidating itself and is, at times, censored by the corporations that own it. And yes, there will be the occasional reporter who is in bed with the administration. But it's there, and, after some foggy years following the invasion of Iraq, it's starting to get angry and do its job. Coverage of

Katrina, Scooter Libby, and Harriet Miers attests to the fact that mainstream political journalists are beginning to remember the crux of their jobs.

We have a battered old warhorse, the Democratic Party, that needs only a bit of TLC and a couple of competent and courageous leaders before it can ride again into the fray.

And we have a disgraced administration that—with its grip on all the levers of power—finally can't blame its own catastrophic foreign and domestic failures on anything but its own policies and methods, even if they'll try to do that for a couple more years.

Best of all, though, we have all the moral and intellectual firepower of guys with names like Madison and Washington and Franklin and Paine—men who believed in the progressive values that this country needs now, more than at any time in recent history since the Great Depression. And they're *our* men, on *our* side.

But what is "our side" anyway? It isn't determined by the "color" of the state you live in, nor is it determined, even, by the party of the candidate for whom you vote. Instead, "our side" is comprised of people with common goals, and, as with most things like this, our friend Thomas Paine puts it best:

"Instead of gazing at each other with suspicious or doubtful curiosity, let each of us, hold out to his neighbour the hearty hand of friendship, and unite in drawing a line, which, like an act of oblivion, shall bury in forgetfulness every former dissention. Let the names of Whig and Tory be extinct; and let none other be heard among us, than those of *a good citizen, an open and resolute friend, and a virtuous supporter of the* RIGHTS *of* MANKIND *and of the* FREE AND INDEPENDENT STATES OF AMERICA."

EPILOGUE

WHEN I THINK OF what political power means to Americans today, I think of watching President Bush's motorcade cross Manhattan, east to west, on Thirty-fourth Street during the Republican National Convention in 2004.

All traffic was barricaded from Thirty-fourth. A wave of police on motorcycles rode out first, followed by long black cars. The presidential limo slid by the assembled crowds packed behind the barricades and cops—Laura, waving at the people through a tinted window, George looking ahead, expressionless. Then black SUVs, then more motorcycles. The whole thing, a sinuous black snake of modern machinery and electronics, power personified.

Thrilling. Scary as hell. And about as distant and remote as the Soviet Politburo up on their little dais during the annual May Day parade of missiles and tanks through downtown Moscow. It's government by shock and awe, government by spectacle.

It was pretty much the opposite of how I felt about government when I was a kid. I grew up in Madison, Wisconsin, in the eighties and early nineties. When I was fourteen or fifteen, my friends and I would—with some regularity—walk into the State Capitol on a day off from school. The group, usually about a dozen kids, would wander the marble corridors and domed rotunda in quiet awe, appreciating the trappings of statehood. After Washington, D.C., and Texas (of course), Wisconsin has the largest of the capitol buildings, and it's an awesome place to ramble through.

Then, after taking our tour, we'd play a game of tag we called "Lock-'n'-Chase." One person would be "it," and would hang out in the Capitol cafeteria. Everyone else would fan out on the Capitol's various floors. If you got tagged, you put on a black armband and became part of the "it" team—last person caught was the winner. Long story short: We would race around like idiots in the State Capitol, the most important building in all of Wisconsin. We dodged aides and legislators in the halls, jumped down flights of marble stairs four or five steps at a time, plunging through groups of bewildered tourists, before a security officer would finally wake up from some back room and gently shoo us out. It usually took about forty-five minutes for us to be evicted.

The State Capitol was *our* building. Our clubhouse. A place where we felt welcome, and safe enough to have free rein of the halls. There was no separation between the halls of power and the people—even if "the people" happened to be teenagers who regularly skipped school assemblies in order to load up on seven-layer burritos at Taco Bell.

In some ways, that was my civic education—growing up in a

state where the seat of government was the same place where we had the farmer's market, where we took our out-of-town friends for casual walks, where we used to play tag. Where there was no aura of power or fear surrounding our "leaders"—they were just people, like us.

I'm not sure what would happen if a group of high school kids tried to play Lock-'n'-Chase in the Wisconsin State Capitol today, in our paranoid, post-9/11 times. (I considered recruiting a batch of kids to try it, but balked at the obvious legal hurdles.) Yet it seems unlikely that things would just slide on by, without charges being filed. Things have gotten uptight as hell; you typically can't protest a campaigning Republican, a Democratic Party convention, or a sitting president without applying for a permit and sitting in a "free-speech" cage several counties away from the actual event.

This is the kind of un-American crap that all of us— conservatives and progressives, liberals and libertarians—need to get together and take down. There are great American arguments out there—the Founding Fathers taught us that you don't have to love your government, and that agreeing with the actions of your leaders is not a prerequisite for being considered a patriot.

But whether or not to give the media and public access to public documents is not one of those arguments, nor is whether or not to have a theocracy, or to ignore the recommendations of scientists and experts in favor of ideologues and fanatics. And it's not up for debate whether the American government should be as transparent and free of fiscal corruption as possible.

Growing up in Wisconsin taught my friends and me to love clean government. When your parents fondly remember Senator William Proxmire (the originator of the "Golden Fleece" award for government waste), your teachers tell you stories about legendary progressive Fighting Bob LaFollette, and you're lucky enough to get to vote for Senator Russ Feingold, you know that political courage isn't an oxymoron—it's a tangible quality that some people actually possess. And until the crony-packed government of Republican governor Tommy Thompson (and the legislative scandals that followed in his wake), state government was renowned for being boring—not crooked.

The pragmatic political courage of my fellow Wisconsinites is what I discovered—and much to my surprise—when reading Ron Chernow's brilliant biography of Alexander Hamilton. Somewhere around page 200, it struck me—"These are my people. The Founding Fathers were progressives, and they would rise from the grave to drive the current administration from office were they physically capable of it. They cared about people, they cared about our essential liberties, and they cared about making government that works."

This isn't to suggest that the legacy of the Founders is exclusively the domain of the modern left. The values of the Founding Fathers have their echoes among modern-day conservatives as well—a fierce belief in the sacredness of the individual, of government's limited reach, of the need to balance national needs with a sense of fiscal responsibility.

But it's the resonance between their ideas and deeds and those of the principled, courageous modern Democratic left that should give us all hope in these otherwise dark days.

The 2006 congressional elections are around the corner, and there is a rising tide of reason that should lift all left-leaning boats in these dark times. Modern Bush conservatism has become seen as tainted, exposed as a rotten edifice built of greed, cronyism, and zealotry clad in the cheap aluminum siding of religious rhetoric. It's a building that needs to be burned to the ground.

Conservatives need to retake the Republican Party, and return it to the pragmatic, small-government, legitimately pro-business (and not mere pro-rich) roots that it has so recently and so catastrophically abandoned. As *Weekly Standard* writer Matt Continetti wrote in the October 1, 2005, edition of *The New York Times*: "[In 1994] DeLay and other Republicans promised 'a new order.' They pledged to drain the swamp that was Washington. Just over a decade later, they find themselves up to their necks in the muck."

And progressives need to get out their copies of the Federalist Papers, and the Constitution, and the writings of Washington and Jefferson and Hamilton, and find the inspiration they need to enter the fight and help put America back on the right track. I hope I've scratched the surface with this book. I hope you'll have read these chapters and emerged thinking: "Maybe he's on to something. I'm going to read Chernow, and Ellis, and Kramnick. I'm going to read Jefferson, and Franklin, and Washington. I'm going to figure out the values that this country was originally founded on. And then I'm going to use those values as an aluminum baseball bat to smash the hell out of the giant black presidential SUV that is currently parked on top of the American flag."

Swing hard, brothers and sisters. Together, we're going to see the reign of witches pass over.

ACKNOWLEDGMENTS

Times are bad. Children no longer obey their parents, and everyone is writing a book.

—Marcus Tullius Cicero

WRITING THIS BOOK was very much like trying to drink from two fire hoses simultaneously. One, the fire hose of American Revolutionary history, expelling everything written or done by the Founding Fathers. The other, the fire hose of contemporary events.

My editor, Ashley Shelby, helped me manage this potentially disastrous situation and you now hold the result in your hands. I'm immeasurably grateful for her patience, professionalism, sense of humor, and formidable talent. It's surprisingly easy to crank out thousands of words of outrage, facts, and analysis. It's far more difficult to mold those words into a readable book.

John Stauber is a fellow Madisonian, and a courageous writer/

reporter whose books on contemporary politics stand among the best available. He's also the guy who helped me get this idea off the ground, and I'm forever grateful.

I also want to thank Al Franken and Billy Kimball, respectively the towering public presence of and secretive mastermind behind *The Al Franken Show.* The show was, for me, a catalyzing experience. After years of fuming about corruption and incompetence in government, they gave me an opportunity to convert steam into energy. Were it not for the show, this book would have never happened. Al and Billy were generous enough to give me a chance to pitch in, and have been more generous and supportive than I had any right to expect.

Two more Madisonians to thank: Ben Wikler, for helping me untangle some of that crazy neocon/Strauss/Nietzsche stuff. Ari Weisbard, for helping me get my head around John Locke.

Matt Hanson, on a purely volunteer basis, fed me volumes of quotes, articles, and ideas that contributed to the hulking whale skeleton of my outline. I'm grateful for his help.

The inordinately talented and generous Derek Evernden helped me with this book's illustrations in a self-sacrificial and heroic manner. Thanks also to illustrators Jim Garmhausen and Charles Fincher, who supplied some laser-sharp strips for this book, omitted, sadly, because of space constraints.

More abstractly, I'm enormously grateful to the editors and writers at the World desk of *The Christian Science Monitor.* Along with their colleagues at organizations such as *The Economist,* the *Los Angeles Times,* BBC, NPR, *Financial Times, The New York Times, The New Yorker,* and *The Washington Post,* they're the best source for Americans who really want to understand what's going on in the world and within their own government. They put their lives on the line with a grace and a good humor that are humbling.

Finally, I'd like to thank my fiancée, Becca Dilley. She got a high-level dose of all the practical problems that an author experiences while finishing a manuscript: paralyzing bouts of insecurity, irregular work hours, paralyzing bouts of vanity, money problems, paralyzing bouts of writer's block, and a fondness for high ABV Quebecois beer. She withstood it all with a minimal level of sarcastic commentary and found the patience and strength to stay by my side and help me write this book.

Thank you, Becca.

THE UNITED STATES CONSTITUTION*

WE THE PEOPLE of the United States, in Order to form a more perfect Union, establish Justice, insure domestic Tranquility, provide for the common defense, promote the general Welfare, and secure the Blessings of Liberty to ourselves and our Posterity, do ordain and establish this Constitution for the United States of America.

ARTICLE. I.

Section. 1.

All legislative Powers herein granted shall be vested in a Congress of the United States, which shall consist of a Senate and House of Representatives.

Section. 2.

The House of Representatives shall be composed of Members chosen every second Year by the People of the several States, and the Electors in each State shall have the Qualifications requisite for Electors of the most numerous Branch of the State Legislature.

No Person shall be a Representative who shall not have attained to the Age of twenty five Years, and been seven Years a Citizen of the United States, and who shall not, when elected, be an Inhabitant of that State in which he shall be chosen.

Representative and direct Taxes shall be apportioned among the several States which may be included within this Union, according to their respective Numbers, which shall

---

*Source: The U.S. National Archives and Records Administration. The text is a transcription of the Constitution in its original form, absent amendments.

be determined by adding to the whole Number of free Persons, including those bound to Service for a Term of Years, and excluding Indians not taxed, three fifths of all other Persons. The actual Enumeration shall be made within three Years after the first Meeting of the Congress of the United States, and within every subsequent Term of ten Years, in such Manner as they shall by Law direct. The Number of Representatives shall not exceed one for every thirty Thousand, but each State shall have at Least one Representative; and until such enumeration shall be made, the State of New Hampshire shall be entitled to chuse three, Massachusetts eight, Rhode-Island and Providence Plantations one, Connecticut five, New-York six, New Jersey four, Pennsylvania eight, Delaware one, Maryland six, Virginia ten, North Carolina five, South Carolina five, and Georgia three.

When vacancies happen in the Representation from any State, the Executive Authority thereof shall issue Writs of Election to fill such Vacancies.

The House of Representatives shall chuse their Speaker and other Officers; and shall have the sole Power of Impeachment.

Section. 3.

The Senate of the United States shall be composed of two Senators from each State, thereof for six Years; and each Senator shall have one Vote.

Immediately after they shall be assembled in Consequence of the first Election, they shall be divided as equally as may be into three Classes. The Seats of the Senators of the first Class shall be vacated at the Expiration of the second Year, of the second Class at the Expiration of the fourth Year, and of the third Class at the Expiration of the sixth Year, so that one third may be chosen every second Year; and if Vacancies happen by Resignation, or otherwise, during the Recess of the Legislature of any State, the Executive thereof may make temporary Appointments until the next Meeting of the Legislature, which shall then fill such Vacancies.

No Person shall be a Senator who shall not have attained to the Age of thirty Years, and been nine Years a Citizen of the United States, and who shall not, when elected, be an Inhabitant of that State for which he shall be chosen.

The Vice President of the United States shall be President of the Senate, but shall have no Vote, unless they be equally divided.

The Senate shall chuse their other Officers, and also a President pro tempore, in the Absence of the Vice President, or when he shall exercise the Office of President of the United States.

The Senate shall have the sole Power to try all Impeachments. When sitting for that

Purpose, they shall be on Oath or Affirmation. When the President of the United States is tried, the Chief Justice shall preside: And no Person shall be convicted without the Concurrence of two thirds of the Members present.

Judgment in Cases of Impeachment shall not extend further than to removal from Office, and disqualification to hold and enjoy any Office of honor, Trust or Profit under the United States: but the Party convicted shall nevertheless be liable and subject to Indictment, Trial, Judgment and Punishment, according to Law.

Section. 4.

The Times, Places and Manner of holding Elections for Senators and Representatives, shall be prescribed in each State by the Legislature thereof; but the Congress may at any time by Law make or alter such Regulations, except as to the Places of chusing Senators.

The Congress shall assemble at least once in every Year, and such Meeting shall be on the first Monday in December, unless they shall by Law appoint a different Day.

Section. 5.

Each House shall be the Judge of the Elections, Returns and Qualifications of its own Members, and a Majority of each shall constitute a Quorum to do Business; but a smaller Number may adjourn from day to day, and may be authorized to compel the Attendance of absent Members, in such Manner, and under such Penalties as each House may provide.

Each House may determine the Rules of its Proceedings, punish its Members for disorderly Behaviour, and, with the Concurrence of two thirds, expel a Member.

Each House shall keep a Journal of its Proceedings, and from time to time publish the same, excepting such Parts as may in their Judgment require Secrecy; and the Yeas and Nays of the Members of either House on any question shall, at the Desire of one fifth of those Present, be entered on the Journal.

Neither House, during the Session of Congress, shall, without the Consent of the other, adjourn for more than three days, nor to any other Place than that in which the two Houses shall be sitting.

Section. 6.

The Senators and Representatives shall receive a Compensation for their Services, to be ascertained by Law, and paid out of the Treasury of the United States. They shall in all Cases, except Treason, Felony and Breach of the Peace, be privileged from Arrest during their Attendance at the Session of their respective Houses, and in going to and returning from the same; and for any Speech or Debate in either House, they shall not be questioned in any other Place.

No Senator or Representative shall, during the Time for which he was elected, be appointed to any civil Office under the Authority of the United States, which shall have been created, or the Emoluments whereof shall have been encreased during such time; and no Person holding any Office under the United States, shall be a Member of either House during his Continuance in Office.

Section. 7.

All Bills for raising Revenue shall originate in the House of Representatives; but the Senate may propose or concur with Amendments as on other Bills.

Every Bill which shall have passed the House of Representatives and the Senate, shall, before it become a Law, be presented to the President of the United States: If he approve he shall sign it, but if not he shall return it, with his Objections to that House in which it shall have originated, who shall enter the Objections at large on their Journal, and proceed to reconsider it. If after such Reconsideration two thirds of that House shall agree to pass the Bill, it shall be sent, together with the Objections, to the other House, by which it shall likewise be reconsidered, and if approved by two thirds of that House, it shall become a Law. But in all such Cases the Votes of both Houses shall be determined by yeas and Nays, and the Names of the Persons voting for and against the Bill shall be entered on the Journal of each House respectively. If any Bill shall not be returned by the President within ten Days (Sundays excepted) after it shall have been presented to him, the Same shall be a Law, in like Manner as if he had signed it, unless the Congress by their Adjournment prevent its Return, in which Case it shall not be a Law.

Every Order, Resolution, or Vote to which the Concurrence of the Senate and House of Representatives may be necessary (except on a question of Adjournment) shall be presented to the President of the United States; and before the Same shall take Effect, shall be approved by him, or being disapproved by him, shall be repassed by two thirds of the Senate and House of Representatives, according to the Rules and Limitations prescribed in the Case of a Bill.

Section. 8.

The Congress shall have Power To lay and collect Taxes, Duties, Imposts and Excises, to pay the Debts and provide for the common Defence and general Welfare of the United States; but all Duties, Imposts and Excises shall be uniform throughout the United States;

To borrow Money on the credit of the United States;

To regulate Commerce with foreign Nations, and among the several States, and with the Indian Tribes;

To establish an uniform Rule of Naturalization, and uniform Laws on the subject of Bankruptcies throughout the United States;

To coin Money, regulate the Value thereof, and of foreign Coin, and fix the Standard of Weights and Measures;

To provide for the Punishment of counterfeiting the Securities and current Coin of the United States;

To establish Post Offices and post Roads;

To promote the Progress of Science and useful Arts, by securing for limited Times to Authors and Inventors the exclusive Right to their respective Writings and Discoveries;

To constitute Tribunals inferior to the supreme Court;

To define and punish Piracies and Felonies committed on the high Seas, and Offences against the Law of Nations;

To declare War, grant Letters of Marque and Reprisal, and make Rules concerning Captures on Land and Water;

To raise and support Armies, but no Appropriation of Money to that Use shall be for a longer Term than two Years;

To provide and maintain a Navy;

To make Rules for the Government and Regulation of the land and naval Forces;

To provide for calling forth the Militia to execute the Laws of the Union, suppress Insurrections and repel Invasions;

To provide for organizing, arming, and disciplining, the Militia, and for governing such Part of them as may be employed in the Service of the United States, reserving to the States respectively, the Appointment of the Officers, and the Authority of training the Militia according to the discipline prescribed by Congress;

To exercise exclusive Legislation in all Cases whatsoever, over such District (not exceeding ten Miles square) as may, by Cession of particular States, and the Acceptance of Congress, become the Seat of the Government of the United States, and to exercise like Authority over all Places purchased by the Consent of the Legislature of the State in which the Same shall be, for the Erection of Forts, Magazines, Arsenals, dock-Yards, and other needful Buildings;—And

To make all Laws which shall be necessary and proper for carrying into Execution the foregoing Powers, and all other Powers vested by this Constitution in the Government of the United States, or in any Department or Officer thereof.

Section. 9.

The Migration or Importation of such Persons as any of the States now existing shall think proper to admit, shall not be prohibited by the Congress prior to the Year one thousand eight hundred and eight, but a Tax or duty may be imposed on such Importation, not exceeding ten dollars for each Person.

The Privilege of the Writ of Habeas Corpus shall not be suspended, unless when in Cases of Rebellion or Invasion the public Safety may require it.

No Bill of Attainder or ex post facto Law shall be passed.

No Capitation, or other direct, Tax shall be laid, unless in Proportion to the Census or enumeration herein before directed to be taken.

No Tax or Duty shall be laid on Articles exported from any State.

No Preference shall be given by any Regulation of Commerce or Revenue to the Ports of one State over those of another; nor shall Vessels bound to, or from, one State, be obliged to enter, clear, or pay Duties in another.

No Money shall be drawn from the Treasury, but in Consequence of Appropriations made by Law; and a regular Statement and Account of the Receipts and Expenditures of all public Money shall be published from time to time.

No Title of Nobility shall be granted by the United States: And no Person holding any Office of Profit or Trust under them, shall, without the Consent of the Congress, accept of any present, Emolument, Office, or Title, of any kind whatever, from any King, Prince, or foreign State.

Section. 10.

No State shall enter into any Treaty, Alliance, or Confederation; grant Letters of Marque and Reprisal; coin Money; emit Bills of Credit; make any Thing but gold and silver Coin a Tender in Payment of Debts; pass any Bill of Attainder, ex post facto Law, or Law impairing the Obligation of Contracts, or grant any Title of Nobility.

No State shall, without the Consent of the Congress, lay any Imposts or Duties on Imports or Exports, except what may be absolutely necessary for executing its inspection Laws: and the net Produce of all Duties and Imposts, laid by any State on Imports or

Exports, shall be for the Use of the Treasury of the United States; and all such Laws shall be subject to the Revision and Controul of the Congress.

No State shall, without the Consent of Congress, lay any Duty of Tonnage, keep Troops, or Ships of War in time of Peace, enter into any Agreement or Compact with another State, or with a foreign Power, or engage in War, unless actually invaded, or in such imminent Danger as will not admit of delay.

ARTICLE. II.

Section. 1.

The executive Power shall be vested in a President of the United States of America. He shall hold his Office during the Term of four Years, and, together with the Vice President, chosen for the same Term, be elected, as follows:

Each State shall appoint, in such Manner as the Legislature thereof may direct, a Number of Electors, equal to the whole Number of Senators and Representatives to which the State may be entitled in the Congress: but no Senator or Representative, or Person holding an Office of Trust or Profit under the United States, shall be appointed an Elector.

The Electors shall meet in their respective States, and vote by Ballot for two Persons, of whom one at least shall not be an Inhabitant of the same State with themselves. And they shall make a List of all the Persons voted for, and of the Number of Votes for each; which List they shall sign and certify, and transmit sealed to the Seat of the Government of the United States, directed to the President of the Senate. The President of the Senate shall, in the Presence of the Senate and House of Representative, open all the Certificates, and the Votes shall then be counted. The person having the greatest Number of Votes shall be the President, if such Number be a Majority of the whole Number of Electors appointed; and if there be more than one who have such Majority, and have an equal Number of Votes, then the House of Representatives shall immediately chuse by Ballot one of them for President; and if no Person have a Majority, then from the five highest on the List the said House shall in like Manner chuse the President. But in chusing the President, the Votes shall be taken by States, the Representation from each State having one Vote; A quorum for this purpose shall consist of a Member or Members from two thirds of the States, and a Majority of all the States shall be necessary to a Choice.

In every Case, after the Choice of the President, the Person having the greatest Number of Votes of the Electors shall be the Vice President. But if there should remain two or more who have equal Votes, the Senate shall chuse from them by Ballot the Vice President.

The Congress may determine the Time of chusing the Electors, and the Day on which they shall give their Votes; which Day shall be the same throughout the United States.

No Person except a natural born Citizen, or a Citizen of the United States, at the time of the Adoption of this Constitution, shall be eligible to the Office of President; neither shall any Person be eligible to that Office who shall not have attained to the Age of thirty five Years, and been fourteen Years a Resident within the United States.

In Case of the Removal of the President from Office, or of his Death, Resignation, or Inability to discharge the Powers and Duties of the said Office, the Same shall devolve on the Vice President, and the Congress may by Law provide for the Case of Removal, Death, Resignation or Inability, both of the President and Vice President, declaring what Officer shall then act as President, and such Officer shall act accordingly, until the Disability be removed, or a President shall be elected.

The President shall, at stated Times, receive for his Services, a Compensation, which shall neither be increased nor diminished during the Period for which he shall have been elected, and he shall not receive within that Period any other Emolument from the United States, or any of them.

Before he enter on the Execution of his Office, he shall take the following Oath or Affirmation:—"I do solemnly swear (or affirm) that I will faithfully execute the Office of President of the United States, and will to the best of my Ability, preserve, protect and defend the Constitution of the United States."

Section. 2.

The President shall be Commander in Chief of the Army and Navy of the United States, and of the Militia of the several States, when called into the actual Service of the United States; he may require the Opinion, in writing, of the principal Officer in each of the executive Departments, upon any Subject relating to the Duties of their respective Offices, and he shall have Power to grant Reprieves and Pardons for Offences against the United States, except in Cases of Impeachment.

He shall have Power, by and with the Advice and Consent of the Senate, to make

Treaties, provided two thirds of the Senators present concur; and he shall nominate, and by and with the Advice and Consent of the Senate, shall appoint Ambassadors, other public Ministers and Consuls, Judges of the supreme Court, and all other Officers of the United States, whose Appointments are not herein otherwise provided for, and which shall be established by Law: but the Congress may by Law vest the Appointment of such inferior Officers, as they think proper, in the President alone, in the Courts of Law, or in the Heads of Departments.

The President shall have Power to fill up all Vacancies that may happen during the Recess of the Senate, by granting Commissions which shall expire at the End of their next Session.

Section. 3.

He shall from time to time give to the Congress Information of the State of the Union, and recommend to their Consideration such Measures as he shall judge necessary and expedient; he may, on extraordinary Occasions, convene both Houses, or either of them, and in Case of Disagreement between them, with Respect to the Time of Adjournment, he may adjourn them to such Time as he shall think proper; he shall receive Ambassadors and other public Ministers; he shall take Care that the Laws be faithfully executed, and shall Commission all the Officers of the United States.

Section. 4.

The President, Vice President and all civil Officers of the United States, shall be removed from Office on Impeachment for, and Conviction of, Treason, Bribery, or other high Crimes and Misdemeanors.

Article. III.

Section. 1.

The judicial Power of the United States shall be vested in one supreme Court, and in such inferior Courts as the Congress may from time to time ordain and establish. The Judges, both of the supreme and inferior Courts, shall hold their Offices during good Behaviour, and shall, at stated Times, receive for their Services a Compensation, which shall not be diminished during their Continuance in Office.

Section. 2.

The judicial Power shall extend to all Cases, in Law and Equity, arising under this Constitution, the Laws of the United States, and Treaties made, or which shall be made, under their Authority;—to all Cases affecting Ambassadors, other public Ministers and Consuls;—to all Cases of admiralty and maritime Jurisdiction;—to Controversies to which the United States shall be a Party;—to Controversies between two or more States;—between Citizens of different States;—between Citizens of the same State claiming Lands under Grants of different States, and between a State, or the Citizens thereof, and foreign States, Citizens or Subjects.

In all Cases affecting Ambassadors, other public Ministers and Consuls, and those in which a State shall be Party, the supreme Court shall have original Jurisdiction. In all the other Cases before mentioned, the supreme Court shall have appellate Jurisdiction, both as to Law and Fact, with such Exceptions, and under such Regulations as the Congress shall make.

The Trial of all Crimes, except in Cases of Impeachment, shall be by Jury; and such Trial shall be held in the State where the said Crimes shall have been committed; but when not committed within any State, the Trial shall be at such Place or Places as the Congress may by Law have directed.

Section. 3.

Treason against the United States, shall consist only in levying War against them, or in adhering to their Enemies, giving them Aid and Comfort. No Person shall be convicted of Treason unless on the Testimony of two Witnesses to the same overt Act, or on Confession in open Court.

The Congress shall have Power to declare the Punishment of Treason, but no Attainder of Treason shall work Corruption of Blood, or Forfeiture except during the Life of the Person attainted.

Article. IV.

Section. 1.

Full Faith and Credit shall be given in each State to the public Acts, Records, and judicial Proceedings of every other State. And the Congress may by general Laws prescribe the Manner in which such Acts, Records and Proceedings shall be proved, and the Effect thereof.

Section. 2.

The Citizens of each State shall be entitled to all Privileges and Immunities of Citizens in the several States.

A Person charged in any State with Treason, Felony, or other Crime, who shall flee from Justice, and be found in another State, shall on Demand of the executive Authority of the State from which he fled, be delivered up, to be removed to the State having Jurisdiction of the Crime.

No Person held to Service or Labour in one State, under the Laws thereof, escaping into another, shall, in Consequence of any Law or Regulation therein, be discharged from such Service or Labour, but shall be delivered up on Claim of the Party to whom such Service or Labour may be due.

Section. 3.

New States may be admitted by the Congress into this Union; but no new State shall be formed or erected within the Jurisdiction of any other State; nor any State be formed by the Junction of two or more States, or Parts of States, without the Consent of the Legislatures of the States concerned as well as of the Congress.

The Congress shall have Power to dispose of and make all needful Rules and Regulations respecting the Territory or other Property belonging to the United States; and nothing in this Constitution shall be so construed as to Prejudice any Claims of the United States, or of any particular State.

Section. 4.

The United States shall guarantee to every State in this Union a Republican Form of Government, and shall protect each of them against Invasion; and on Application of the Legislature, or of the Executive (when the Legislature cannot be convened), against domestic Violence.

Article. V.

The Congress, whenever two thirds of both Houses shall deem it necessary, shall propose Amendments to this Constitution, or, on the Application of the Legislatures of two thirds of the several States, shall call a Convention for proposing Amendments, which, in either Case, shall be valid to all Intents and Purposes, as Part of this Constitution, when ratified by the Legislatures of three fourths of the several States, or by Conventions in three fourths thereof, as the one or the other Mode of Ratification may be proposed by the Congress; Provided that no Amendment which may be made prior to the Year One thousand eight hundred and eight shall in any Manner affect the first and fourth Clauses in the Ninth Section of the first Article; and that no State, without its Consent, shall be deprived of its equal Suffrage in the Senate.

ARTICLE. VI.

All Debts contracted and Engagements entered into, before the Adoption of this Constitution, shall be as valid against the United States under this Constitution, as under the Confederation.

This Constitution, and the Laws of the United States which shall be made in Pursuance thereof; and all Treaties made, or which shall be made, under the Authority of the United States, shall be the supreme Law of the Land; and the Judges in every State shall be bound thereby, any Thing in the Constitution or Laws of any State to the Contrary notwithstanding.

The Senators and Representatives before mentioned, and the Members of the several State Legislatures, and all executive and judicial Officers, both of the United States and of the several States, shall be bound by Oath or Affirmation, to support this Constitution; but no religious Test shall ever be required as a Qualification to any Office or public Trust under the United States.

ARTICLE. VII.

The Ratification of the Conventions of nine States, shall be sufficient for the Establishment of this Constitution between the States so ratifying the Same.

The Word, "the," being interlined between the seventh and eighth Lines of the first Page, the Word "Thirty" being partly written on an Erazure in the fifteenth Line of the first Page, The Words "is tried" being interlined between the thirty second and thirty third Lines of the first Page and the Word "the" being interlined between the forty third and forty fourth Lines of the second Page.

Attest William Jackson Secretary

Done in Convention by the Unanimous Consent of the States present the Seventeenth Day of September in the Year of our Lord one thousand seven hundred and Eighty seven and of the Independence of the United States of America the Twelfth In witness whereof We have hereunto subscribed our Names,

G°. Washington
Presidt and deputy from Virginia

Delaware
Geo: Read
Gunning Bedford jun
John Dickinson
Richard Bassett
Jaco: Broom

Maryland
James McHenry
Dan of St Thos. Jenifer
Danl. Carroll

Virginia
John Blair
James Madison Jr.

North Carolina
Wm. Blount
Richd. Dobbs Spaight
Hu Williamson

South Carolina
J. Rutledge
Charles Cotesworth Pinckney
Charles Pinckney
Pierce Butler

Georgia
William Few
Abr Baldwin

New Hampshire
John Langdon
Nicholas Gilman

Massachusetts
Nathaniel Gorham
Rufus King

Connecticut
Wm. Saml. Johnson
Roger Sherman

New York
Alexander Hamilton

New Jersey
Wil: Livingston
David Brearley
Wm. Paterson
Jona: Dayton

Pennsylvania
B Franklin
Thomas Mifflin
Robt. Morris
Geo. Clymer
Thos. FitzSimons
Jared Ingersoll
James Wilson

SELECTED BIBLIOGRAPHY

This book is principally a comparison of current events—mostly as reported by mainstream contemporary news media—with the original words and deeds of the Founding Fathers. I owe a special debt to Ron Chernow for his lucid and expansive biography of Alexander Hamilton, which was the original inspiration for this book. And I owe another debt to the publishers of the Library of America series of books that so elegantly and comprehensively preserves the writings of America's founders and framers.

I also relied heavily on the reporting of the BBC, *The Washington Post, The New York Times, The Economist, The Christian Science Monitor,* the *Los Angeles Times,* and numerous other journals of news and opinion. I'm also in debt to a raft of excellent websites, including Talking Points Memo, DailyKos, Juan Cole's Informed Comment, and SourceWatch.

Bailyn, Bernard, ed. *The Debate on the Constitution: Part One and Part Two.* New York: The Library of America, 1993.

Boorstein, Daniel J. *An American Primer.* New York: Meridian, 1995.

Brogan, Hugh. *The Penguin History of the U.S.A.* New York: Penguin, 2001.

Chernow, Ron. *Alexander Hamilton.* New York: Penguin, 2004.

Clarke, Richard A. *Against All Enemies.* New York: The Free Press, 2004.

Dean, John W. *Worse Than Watergate.* New York: Little, Brown, 2004.

Ellis, Joseph J. *Founding Brothers.* New York: Knopf, 2001.

Ellis, Joseph J. *His Excellency, George Washington.* New York: Knopf, 2004.

Foner, Eric, ed. *Paine: Collected Writings.* New York: The Library of America, 1995.

Franken, Al. *Lies and the Lying Liars Who Tell Them.* New York: Dutton, 2003.

Franken, Al. *The Truth, with Jokes.* New York: Dutton, 2005.

Johnston, David Cay. *Perfectly Legal.* New York: Portfolio, 2003.

Kaye, Harvey J. *Thomas Paine and the Promise of America.* New York: Hill and Wang, 2005.

Kramnick, Isaac, and R. Laurence Moore. *The Godless Constitution: The Case Against Religious Correctness.* New York: Norton, 1997.

Kramnick, Isaac, ed. *The Portable Enlightenment Reader.* New York: Penguin, 1995.

Lemisch, L. Jesse, ed. *Benjamin Franklin: The Autobiography and Other Writings.* New York: Signet, 2001.

Madison, James, Alexander Hamilton, and John Jay. *The Federalist Papers.* New York: Penguin, 1997.

Needleman, Jacob. *The American Soul.* New York: Tarcher, 2002.

Paine, Thomas. *Common Sense, The Rights of Man, and Other Essential Writings of Thomas Paine.* New York: Meridian, 1984.

Peterson, Merrill D., ed. *Jefferson: Writings.* New York: The Library of America, 1984.

Rakove, Jack N., ed. *Madison: Writings.* New York: The Library of America, 1999.

Rampton, Sheldon, and John Stauber. *Banana Republicans.* New York: Tarcher, 2004.

Rampton, Sheldon, and John Stauber. *Weapons of Mass Deception.* New York: Tarcher, 2003.

Rhodehamel, John, ed. *Washington: Writings.* New York: The Library of America, 1997.

Roberts, Cokie. *Founding Mothers.* New York: Perennial, 2005.

Shuffleton, Frank C., ed. *Thomas Jefferson: Notes on the State of Virginia.* New York: Penguin, 1999.

Tocqueville, Alexis de. *Democracy in America.* New York: Penguin, 2003.

NOTES

1. CNN, December 18, 2000.

2. Merrill D. Peterson, ed., *Jefferson: Writings* (New York: The Library of America, 1984), 71–72.

3. *Today*, Aug. 30, 2004.

4. *Slate*, "Uncivil Liberties: Why Won't the Bush Administration Obey the Law?" by Dahlia Lithwick, Dec. 21, 2005.

5. Thomas Paine, *Common Sense, The Rights of Man, and Other Essential Writings of Thomas Paine* (New York: Meridian, 1984): 255.

6. Thomas Paine, *The Age of Reason*, Part First, Section II.

7. Paine, *Common Sense, The Crisis*, 85.

8. John Rhodehamel, ed., *Washington: Writings* (New York: The Library of America, 1997), 533.

9. Ibid., 757.

10. Peterson, *Jefferson: Writings*, 521.

11. NPR, "On the Media," Jan. 13, 2001.

12. SourceWatch.org: "Covert Propaganda."

13. CBS News, "Investigators Eye Education Dept.," Oct. 14, 2005.

14. Letter from Rep. Henry Waxman and eleven other congressmen, Oct. 21, 2002, expressing concern over "a pattern of events at the Department of Health and Human Services (HHS) suggesting that scientific decision making is being subverted by ideology and that scientific information that does not fit the Administration's political agenda is being suppressed."

15. *The Hill*, "GAO Calls Medicare Video News Releases Illegal Propaganda," by Michael Gerber, May 20, 2004.

16. *The New York Times,* "U.S. Is Said to Pay to Plant Articles in Iraq Papers," by Jeff Gerth and Scott Shane, Dec. 1, 2005.

17. *Newsweek,* "How Bush Blew It," by Evan Thomas, Sept. 19, 2005.

18. *The New York Times,* "President, Citing Executive Privilege, Indicates He'll Reject Requests for Counsel's Documents," by Richard W. Stevenson, Oct. 5, 2005.

19. *Secrecy News* (FAS Project on Government Secrecy), volume 2005, issue no. 71 (July 28, 2005).

20. U.S. Dept. of Justice website FOIA post, Oct. 15, 2001.

21. Bloomberg, "Bush Cronyism Weakens Government Agencies," September 30, 2005.

22. Ibid.

23. *The New York Times,* "Bring Back Warren Harding," by Frank Rich, Sept. 25, 2005.

24. Peterson, *Jefferson: Writings,* 966–67.

25. *The Washington Post,* "House GOP Leaders Name Loyalist to Replace Ethics Chief," by Mike Allen, Feb. 3, 2005.

26. *The Boston Globe,* "Truth Trumped," Sept. 6, 2005.

27. CNN, *American Morning,* March 22, 2004.

28. CBS, *60 Minutes,* "Bush Sought 'Way' to Invade Iraq?" Jan. 11, 2004.

29. *Forbes,* "The Next Maestro," by Matthew Suibel with Kenneth Black, Oct. 31, 2005.

30. CBS News, "Ex–Bush Aide: Terror War a Bust," June 16, 2003.

31. Ron Chernow, *Alexander Hamilton* (New York: Penguin, 2004), 115.

32. Phone interview with the author, Aug. 30, 2005.

33. Chernow, *Alexander Hamilton,* 235.

34. *Federalist No. 10.*

35. John Adams, letter to John Quincy Adams, Nov. 13, 1816, in Isaac Kramnick and R. Laurence Moore, *The Godless Constitution* (New York: Norton, 1997), 102.

36. Kramnick and Moore, *The Godless Constitution,* 91.

37. *Los Angeles Times,* "State of the 'Vision Thing,'" by Arthur M. Schlesinger, Jr., Jan. 21, 2004.

38. CBS News/Associated Press, "Top General: Could It Be Satan?" Oct. 17, 2003.

39. Ibid.

40. NBC News, "Top Terrorist Hunter's Divisive Views," by Lisa Myers and NBC investigative unit, Oct. 15, 2003.

41. William Dembski, *The Design Revolution* (Downer's Grove, IL: Intervarsity Press, 2004), 27.

42. "The Establishment Clause, Religion and the First Amendment," by Leonard W. Levy, 124.

43. *The New York Times,* "Report Details F.D.A. Rejection of Next-Day Pill," by Gardiner Harris, Nov. 15, 2005.

44. *The Washington Post,* "Debate Rages on Use of Cervical Cancer Vaccine," by Rob Stein, Oct. 31, 2005.

45. CNN.com, "Rove: Conservatives 'Will Win' Debate Over Judges," Nov. 11, 2005.

46. Associated Press, "Author Tom Clancy Criticizes Iraq War," May 24, 2004.

47. Benjamin Franklin, letter to Benjamin Vaughan, Oct. 24, 1788.

48. Chernow, *Alexander Hamilton,* 134.

49. *Newsweek,* "Bush in the Bubble," by Evan Thomas and Richard Wolffe, Dec. 19, 2005.

50. Ibid.

51. Republican presidential primary TV debate, Greater Des Moines Civic Center, Iowa, Dec. 13, 1999, as reported in *St. Petersburg Times,* Jan. 16, 2005.

52. Letter to artist John Trumbull, Feb. 15, 1789, in Peterson, *Jefferson: Writings.* You can see a great copy of this letter online: http://www.loc.gov/exhibits/jefferson/images/vc18.jpg.

53. Letter to Hamilton's friend John Laurens, April 1779, in Chernow, *Alexander Hamilton,* 127.

54. Introduction to *Benjamin Franklin: The Autobiography and Other Writings,* ed. L. Jesse Lemisch (New York: Signet, 2001), ix.

55. Rhodehamel, *Washington: Writings,* 555–556.

56. Kramnick and Moore, *The Godless Constitution,* 105.

57. Letter to Mrs. Samuel H. Smith, Aug. 6, 1816, in Peterson, *Jefferson: Writings,* 1404.

58. Jane Mayer, "Outsourcing Terror," *The New Yorker,* Feb. 14, 2005.

59. PBS, *Frontline,* "The Torture Question," Oct. 15, 2005.

60. Ibid.

61. James Madison Museum website, "James Madison and Slavery" (http://www.james madisonmus.org/resources/slavery.htm).

62. Second Annual Message to Congress, 1790, in Rhodehamel, *Washington: Writings,* 770.

63. Letter to David Humphreys, July 20, 1791, in Rhodehamel, *Washington: Writings,* 779.

64. Letter to Charles Carroll, April 15, 1791, in Peterson, *Jefferson: Writings,* 977.

65. Letter to Thomas Gage, Aug. 19, 1775, in Rhodehamel, *Washington: Writings,* 182.

66. *The New York Times,* "Who We Are," by Bob Herbert, Aug. 1, 2005.

67. Chernow, *Alexander Hamilton,* 267.

68. Letter to Marquis de Lafayette, June 19, 1788, in Rhodehamel, *Washington: Writings,* 684.

69. Bill Moyers, "Acceptance of America's Future Lifetime Leadership Award," at the Take Back America Conference, June 4, 2003.

70. Harvey J. Kaye, *Thomas Paine and the Promise of America* (New York: Hill and Wang, 2005), 220.

INDEX

James Norton is a producer for *The Al Franken Show*. A native Wisconsinite, he attended UW-Madison, where he was editor in chief of *The Daily Cardinal*; he graduated in 1999 with a B.A. in history. He went on to *The Christian Science Monitor,* where he worked at csmonitor.com before serving as Middle East editor for the print edition.

A cofounder of *Flak* (www.flakmag.com), a daily on-line magazine, he continues to write and edit for it despite its extreme unprofitability.

Norton lives in Minneapolis with his fiancée, Becca Dilley.